BEGINNING
LEVEL 1

Choral
Connections

Mixed Voices

Glencoe
McGraw-Hill

New York, New York   Columbus, Ohio   Woodland Hills, California   Peoria, Illinois

Cover Photos: Paul Chen/Masterfile and Eureka Collection/SuperStock, Inc.

Glencoe/McGraw-Hill

A Division of The McGraw·Hill Companies

Send all inquiries to
Glencoe/McGraw-Hill
21600 Oxnard Street, Suite 500
Woodland Hills, CA 91367

ISBN 0-02-655605-7 (Student's Edition)
ISBN 0-02-655606-5 (Teacher's Wraparound Edition)

Printed in the United States of America.

2 3 4 5 6 7 8 9   045   05 04 03 02 01 00 99

Meet the Authors

Mollie G. Tower, Senior Author

As Coordinator of Choral and General Music of the Austin Independent School District for 21 years, Mollie Tower was recently nominated as "Administrator of the Year." She is very active in international, national, regional, and state music educators' organizations. Ms. Tower was contributing author, consultant, and reviewer for the elementary textbook programs, *Share the Music* and *Music and You.* Senior author of *Música para todos, Primary and Intermediate Dual Language Handbooks for Music Teachers*, she has also written and consulted for many other publications. A longtime advocate for music education, Mollie is a popular clinician who conducts workshops across the country.

Marc Erck
Choir Director

Marc Erck has more than 12 years of choral directing experience. He received his Bachelor's of Music Education from Southwestern University. Marc is currently the director of choirs at Hill Country Middle School in the Eanes Independent School District and Choir Director at University United Methodist Church in Austin, Texas. An adjudicator and clinician, Marc is a member of the Texas Music Adjudicators Association, Texas Music Educators Association, Texas Choral Directors Association, and American Choral Directors Association.

Ruth Phillips
Choir Director

Ruth Phillips has taught choral music in junior high and middle school for 21 years in both the Dallas/Fort Worth area and in San Marcos, Texas. She spent 15 years in the San Marcos CISD teaching junior high choral music. Her choirs received many awards and sweepstakes ratings through the years. She is a clinician, UIL judge, and a member of Texas Music Educators Association, Texas Choral Directors Association, and National Choral Directors Association. Ms. Phillips received a Bachelor of Science degree in All Level Music Education from McMurry University in Abilene, Texas.

Linda S. Wyatt
Choir Director

With 29 years of choir directing experience, Linda S. Wyatt is presently Director of Choirs at Murchison Middle School in Austin, Texas. After receiving her Bachelor of Music Education degree from Southwest Texas State University, she taught at John Marshall High School and Sul Ross Middle School in San Antonio. She is a member of Texas Choral Directors Association and Texas Music Educators Association. Linda serves as the Department Chair and Curriculum Specialist at Murchison Middle School.

Consulting Author

Dr. Susan Snyder has taught all levels of vocal music over the last 25 years. She holds a B.S. in music education from the University of Connecticut and an M.A. from Montclair State College. She holds a PhD. in curriculum and instruction from the University of Connecticut and advanced professional certificates from Memphis State University and the University of Minnesota. Teaching at Hunter College and City University of New York, Dr. Snyder was coordinating author of the elementary music program, *Share the Music*, and a consultant on *Music and You*. She has published many articles on music education and integrated curriculum and is an active clinician and master teacher.

Consultants

Choral Music
Stephan P. Barnicle
Choir Director
Simsbury High School
Simsbury, Connecticut

Vocal Development, Music Literacy
Katherine Saltzer Hickey, D.M.A.
University of California at Los Angeles
Los Angeles, California
Choir Director
Pacific Chorale Children's Choruses
Irvine, California

Music History
Dr. Kermit Peters
University of Nebraska at Omaha
College of Fine Arts
Department of Music
Omaha, Nebraska

Contributors/Teacher Reviewers

Dr. Anton Armstrong
Music Director and Conductor, St. Olaf Choir
St. Olaf College
Northfield, Minnesota

Jeanne Julseth-Heinrich
Choir Director
James Madison Middle School
Appleton, Wisconsin

Caroline Lyon
Ethnomusicologist
University of Texas at Austin
Austin, Texas

Caroline Minear
Supervisor
Orange County School District
Orlando, Florida

Judy Roberts
Choir Director
Central Junior High School
Moore, Oklahoma

Dr. A. Byron Smith
Choir Director
Lincoln High School
Tallahassee, Florida

Table of Contents

ADDITIONAL PERFORMANCE SELECTIONS

CHORAL MUSIC TERMS

Preparatory Material

Notes and Note Values

1 Whole Note	
equals	
2 Half Notes	
equal	
4 Quarter Notes	
equal	
8 Eighth Notes	
equal	
16 Sixteenth Notes	

Rests and Rest Values

1 Whole Rest	
equals	
2 Half Rests	
equal	
4 Quarter Rests	
equal	
8 Eighth Rests	
equal	
16 Sixteenth Rests	

Rhythm Challenge in 4/4 Meter

Directions: Accurately count and/or perform the following rhythms without stopping!

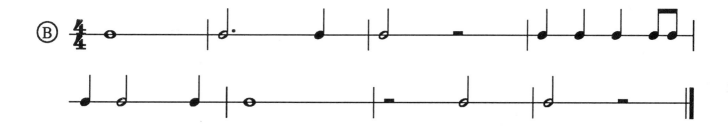

Rhythm Challenge in 6/8 Meter

Directions: Accurately count and/or perform the following rhythms without stopping!

Asymmetric Meter

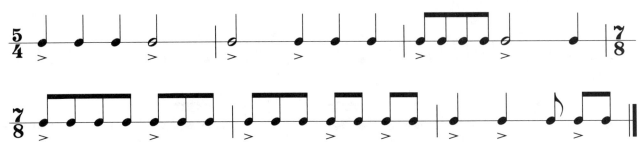

Breathing Mechanics

Singing well requires good breath control. Support for singing comes from correct use of the breathing mechanism. Deep, controlled breathing is needed to sustain long phrases in one breath. Also, correct breathing will support higher, more difficult passages.

Posture
Posture is very important in breath support.
- Keep your body relaxed, but your backbone straight.
- To stretch your back: Bend over and slowly roll your back upward until you are standing straight again. Do this several times.
- Hold your rib cage high, but keep your shoulders low and relaxed.
- Facing front, keep your head level. Imagine you are suspended by a string attached to the very top of your head.
- When you stand, keep your knees relaxed and do not "lock" them by pushing them all the way back. Keep your feet slightly apart.
- When you sit, keep both feet flat on the floor and sit forward in your chair.

Inhaling
- Expand the lungs out and down, pushing the diaphragm muscle down.
- Inhale silently without gasping or making any other noise.
- Imagine taking a cool sip of air through a straw.
- Expand your entire waistline, keeping the shoulders low and relaxed.

Breath Control
To help you develop breath control do the following:
- Hold one finger about six inches from your mouth imagining that your finger is a birthday candle. Now blow out a steady stream of air to blow out the flame of the candle.

Summary

STANDING
Feet slightly apart
Knees relaxed
Backbone straight
Rib cage high
Shoulders low
Head level

SITTING
Feet on the floor
Sit on edge of chair
Backbone straight
Rib cage high
Shoulders low
Head level

Solfège and Hand Signs

Solfège is a system designed to match notes on the staff with specific interval relationships. Hand signs provide additional reinforcement of the pitch relationships.

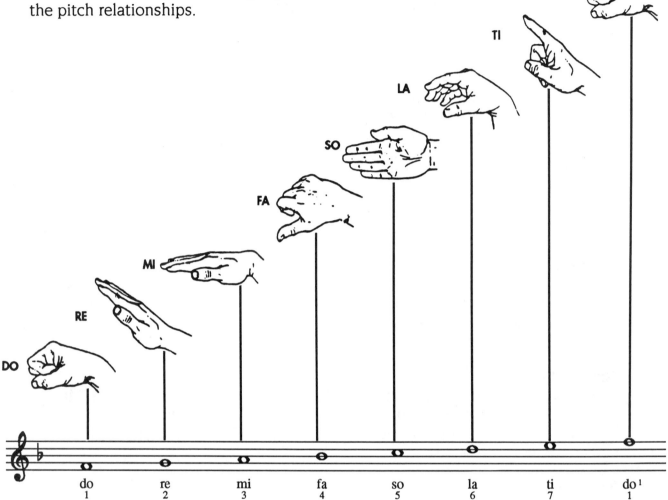

Frequently Found Intervals

An interval is the distance between two notes.

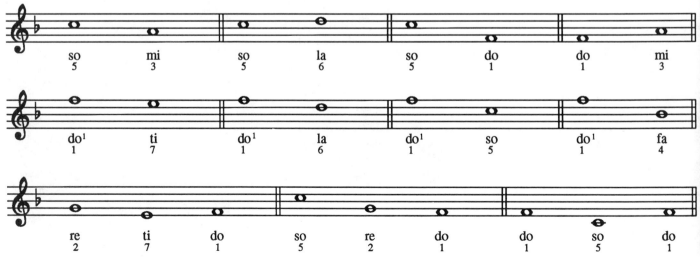

Pitch Challenge

Directions: Accurately sing each measure on solfège using hand signs and without stopping! During the measure of rest, look ahead to the next challenge.

Lessons

LESSON 1

Bound for Jubilee

COMPOSER: *Joyce Elaine Eilers*
TEXT: *Joyce Elaine Eilers*

CHORAL MUSIC TERMS

chord

four-part singing

melodic movement in thirds

melodic stepwise movement

unison

VOICING

SATB

PERFORMANCE STYLE

Spirited

A cappella

FOCUS

- Identify notes moving stepwise and in thirds.
- Sing in four parts.

Warming Up

 Vocal Warm-Up

Sing this warm-up exercise using solfège syllables *do, re, mi, fa,* and *so* or numbers. Repeat the warm-up pattern, beginning one step higher each time. Decide which notes move up or down stepwise, and which move in thirds.

Continue up by half steps.

2 *Choral Connections Level 1 Mixed Voices*

Sight-Singing

Sight-sing these parts using solfège syllables or numbers. Look at and listen to the beginning and end of this exercise. How is the ending different? Use the terms *unison* and *chord* in your comparison.

 # Singing: "Bound for Jubilee"

What do you think the word *jubilee* means?

Jubilee comes from the Hebrew language. In Biblical times, it was a year of celebration that came about every 50 years. During that time there was no farming, and all slaves were freed and their lands restored. During the slavery period in the United States, the term was associated with liberation from bondage, and often had the same meaning as heaven.

Now turn to the music for "Bound for Jubilee" on page 4.

| **HOW DID YOU DO?** ? | Think about your performance of the Vocal Warm-Up, Sight-Singing, and "Bound for Jubilee." 1. What did you do well? 2. Where do you need more work? | 3. How might you demonstrate what you have learned to your classmates or teacher? 4. Explain what you enjoyed most about this lesson. |

Bound for Jubilee

Words and Music by
JOYCE ELAINE EILERS

Mixed Chorus, SATB, A cappella

Oh my broth - er, won't you come with me?
Oh my broth - er, won't you come with me?
Oh my broth - er, won't you come with me?
Oh my broth - er, won't you come with me?

Oh my sis - ter, you must come to - day.
Oh my sis - ter, you must come to - day.
Oh my sis - ter, you must come to - day. _____
Oh my sis - ter, you must come to - day.

LESSON 2

A Red, Red Rose

COMPOSER: *Daniel Burton*
TEXT: *Robert Burns (1759–1796)*

CHORAL MUSIC TERMS

part independence
solfège syllables
soprano, alto, bass
steady beat
text

VOICING

SAB

PERFORMANCE STYLE

Tenderly and expressively
A cappella

FOCUS

- Read and clap rhythms from three staves, maintaining part independence.
- Sing in three parts using solfège syllables, numbers, or text.

Warming Up

Rhythm Drill

Clap the following exercise in 2/4 meter as someone keeps a steady beat. Try each part separately. Then in three groups, clap all three lines at the same time. Listen carefully to your beat keeper. Find three different sounding claps for the three lines.

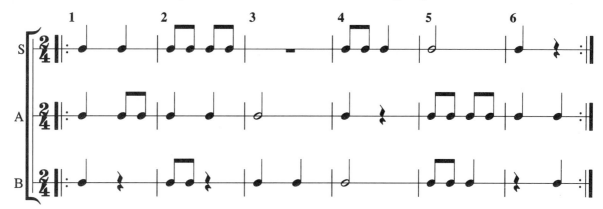

Vocal Warm-up

Sing the chord drill using solfège.

Lesson 2: A Red, Red Rose **11**

Sight-Singing

Sight-sing these parts using solfège syllables or numbers. Find the measures in "A Red, Red Rose" that are similar. Are they the same? If not, what's different?

 # Singing: "A Red, Red Rose"

Do you know what a *round* is?

A *round* is one melody with two or more parts beginning the melody at different times. The result is harmony created by the layering of pitches.

Sing a round of your choice. How many different melodies are being sung? How is each part different? How do you keep singing with your section? Listen to "A Red, Red Rose." What parts sound like a round?

Now turn to the music for "A Red, Red Rose" on page 13.

| **HOW DID YOU DO?** ? | Think about your performance of the Rhythm Drill, Sight-Singing, and "A Red, Red Rose."
 1. What did you do well?
 2. Where do you need more work? | 3. Could you perform the rhythm or sight-singing exercise with only six performers—two on each part?
 4. What did you enjoy most about this lesson? |

A Red, Red Rose

Robert Burns (1759–1796)
Daniel Burton

SAB, A cappella

Used with permissions 1995/96.

LESSON 3

Over There

COMPOSER: *Jerry Ray*
TEXT: *Jerry Ray*

CHORAL MUSIC TERMS

cambiata voice

key signature

phrase

scale

syncopation

VOICING

SAB

PERFORMANCE STYLE

Syncopated

Accompanied by piano

FOCUS

• Sight-sing in different keys using solfège.

• Sight-sing syncopated rhythms.

Warming Up

 Vocal Warm-Up

Sing the following scales in unison with solfège or numbers. Sing the scale in C major using rhythm pattern 1. Sing the whole rhythm pattern on each pitch before moving to the next one. Repeat this with the scale in D♭ major, using rhythm pattern 2.

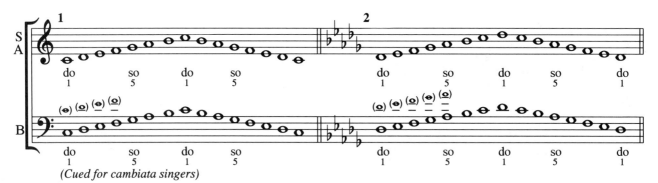

(Cued for cambiata singers)

Clap the following exercise in 4/4 meter as someone keeps a steady beat. Clap each line separately. Then in two groups clap the two lines at one time paying close attention to the syncopated rhythms in line 2.

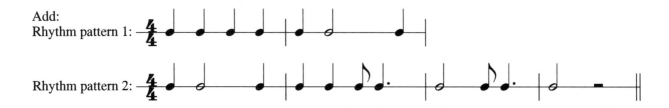

Sight-Singing

Sing each phrase using solfège and hand signs. Notice the key changes. Do you recognize either one of the rhythm patterns from the warm-up activity in this exercise?

 Singing: "Over There"

You can improve your sight-singing skills if you learn to watch for clues. The key signature (the number of sharps or flats at the beginning of each staff) tells you what key to sing in. *Do* is on a different pitch in each key.

Now turn to the music for "Over There" on page 22.

HOW DID YOU DO?

?

The more you read, the more rhythm and melody patterns will seem familiar. Think about your experiences with "Over There."
1. What did you learn that was new?
2. What do you need to know more about?
3. Can you point to two examples of syncopation and the different key signatures in "Over There"? Can you name the keys that each key signature indicates?
4. What are some of the qualities of this piece that reflect a spiritual style?
5. Tell one thing you enjoyed about this lesson.

Over There

Words and Music by
JERRY RAY

SAB with Piano

I'm a - gon - na lay down my bur - dens o - ver

there, o - ver there. Let me take my bur - dens o - ver

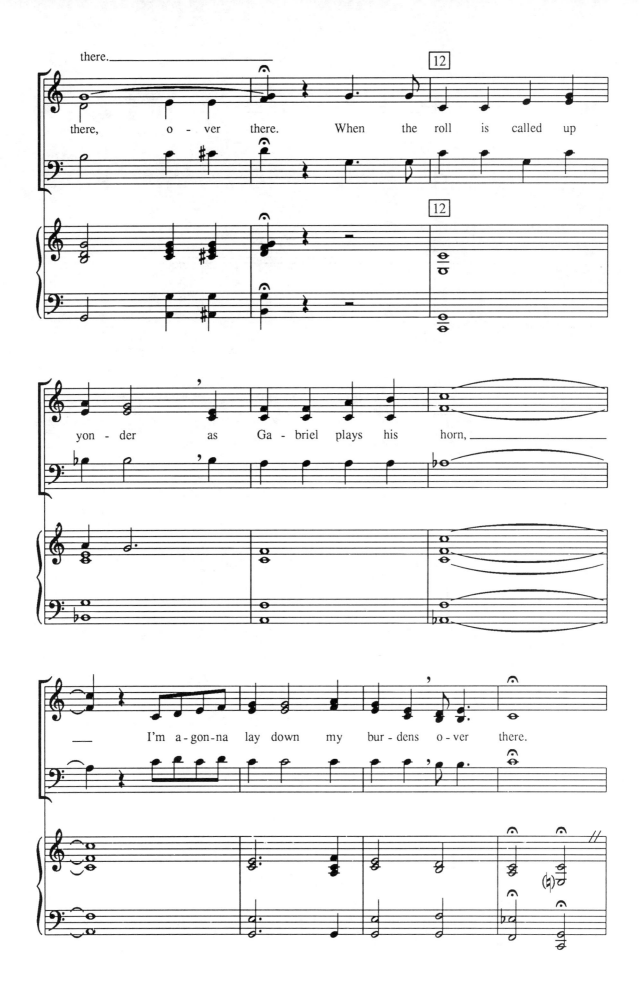

lay down my trou - bles o - ver there, o - ver there.

Let me take my trou - bles o - ver there, o - ver

there. When the roll is called up yon - der as

down.   O - ver there,   when I

66

hear that trum-pet   sound.   O - ver there,   but

66

not be - fore my   time. _____   When   the

LESSON 4

Dare to Dream!

COMPOSER: *Niel Lorenz*
TEXT: *Mary Lynn Lightfoot*

CHORAL MUSIC TERMS
staggered entrances
stepwise movement

VOICING
SAB

PERFORMANCE STYLE
With feeling
Accompanied by piano

FOCUS
- Read stepwise passages with solfège and hand signs.
- Recognize and sing staggered entrances.

Warming Up

 Vocal Warm-Up
Sing each scale and the tonic chord using solfège syllables and hand signs or numbers. Repeat each, moving up by half steps. Be sure to assume singing posture, take a deep breath, and sing with an open tone.

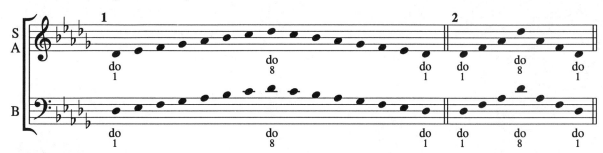

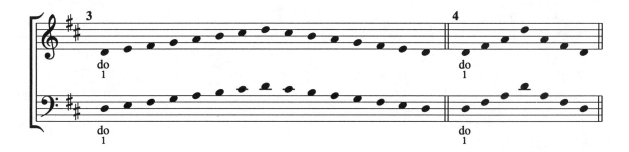

Sight-Singing

Sing this phrase using solfège and hand signs. Notice the staggered entrance. Where does the melody move stepwise in your part?

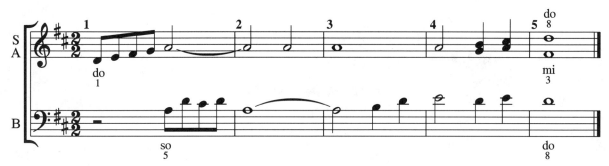

Singing: "Dare to Dream!"

What is your dream? Do you work to make it come true?

Developing skills requires hard work and practice. Whether you are practicing creative writing, sports, or sight-singing, you have to keep working and trying if you're going to succeed.

A Staggered Entrance Game

Count from 1 to 10. Sopranos stand on 1, 5, and 10. Altos stand on 2 and 6. Baritones stand on 3 and 9. Sit on all other numbers. Can you tell what a *staggered entrance* might be?

Now turn to the music for "Dare to Dream!" on page 35.

HOW DID YOU DO?

?
?

It is important to dream about your goals in life. However, if you really have the dream of becoming a good musician, it takes practice. Think about your experiences with "Dare to Dream!"
1. What can you tell about this piece?
2. At which skills are you improving? How do you know?

3. Can you sight-sing your part to "Dare to Dream!"? Which part is easy? Where is it difficult? What do you do differently during the difficult passages than the easy ones?
4. Did you recognize where your staggered entrance occurs?
5. What did you enjoy most about this lesson?

Dare to Dream!

Niel Lorenz
Mary Lynn Lightfoot

Three-part Mixed Chorus and Piano

Reproduced by permission. Permit # 275772.

when you have a dream, though hard work it may

seem! Dare to go! Dare to know! Dare to try! Dare to

fly!

Work_ hard for your dream! Dare to be all you can be!

Work hard, work hard for your dream!

unis. *poco rit.* *molto rit.*

Dare to go! Dare to know!

poco rit. *molto rit.*

See all you can see! Dare to try! Dare to fly!

poco rit. *molto rit.*

49 *unis.* *a tempo*

If you have a dream, _____ see it through! _____

a tempo

If you have a dream, _____ see it

49

f a tempo

LESSON 5

The Tiger

COMPOSER: *Sherri Porterfield*
TEXT: *William Blake* (1757–1827)

CHORAL MUSIC TERMS
repetitive entrances
6/8 meter
symbol

VOICING
SAB

PERFORMANCE STYLE
With intensity
Accompanied by piano

FOCUS
- Read rhythms in 6/8 meters.
- Locate repetitive entrances.

Warming Up

Rhythm Drill

Clap each line separately. Choose a sound for each line, for example: line 1, stand and step in place; line 2, pat your legs; line 3, clap; line 4, "sizzle the rhythm" using a *ts* sound. Each group starts on one of the lines, then reads through the whole piece twice and stops.

Vocal Warm-Up
Sing the exercise below using solfège.

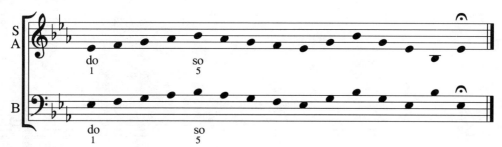

 Sight-Singing
Sing this phrase using solfège and hand signs. Notice the symbol for "no breath."

 # Singing: "The Tiger"

A symbol is something that represents something else. Notation is a symbol system, and so are words.

What do you think the tiger symbolizes in William Blake's poetry, "The Tiger" page 44? Does everyone have the same idea, or are symbols personal and individual?

Now turn and perform the music for "The Tiger" on page 44.

HOW DID YOU DO?

?
?

A tiger can be considered a symbol of destruction, or a bold and daring creature. Which were you during this lesson? Think about your experiences with "The Tiger."
1. Do you understand 6/8 meter?
2. How was your sight-singing? What did you do really well? What still needs more practice?

3. Do you think the composer did a good job of setting William Blake's poem "The Tiger"? What musical tools did she use effectively? Would you have done anything differently?

The Tiger

COMPOSER: Sherri Porterfield
TEXT: William Blake (1757–1827)

Three-part Mixed, Accompanied

Ti - ger! Ti - ger! burn-ing bright - ly in the for - ests

wings dare he as - pire?   What the hand dare seize the fire?___

What the chain?   In   what fur - nace

What the ham - mer?___

was   thy   brain?_____   What the an - vil?   What dread grasp

dare   its dead - ly ter   -   rors   clasp?

When the   stars   threw down   their   spears_____   and

wa - tered heav - en   with their tears,___ did He smile His work to

LESSON 6

Shalom, My Friends

Based on a traditional Hebrew melody
TEXT: Douglas E. Wagner

CHORAL MUSIC TERMS

la tonal center

minor mode

relationships between parts

tuning chords

VOICING
SAB

PERFORMANCE STYLE
Moderate
Accompanied by piano

FOCUS
- Sight-sing pitches in D minor.
- Describe different relationships between vocal parts.
- Sight-sing a piece in three parts, using solfège or text.

Warming Up

Vocal Warm-Up

Sing these examples using solfège syllables and hand signs or numbers, listening for balance, tuning, and blend. Is *do* the tonal center in each of these examples?

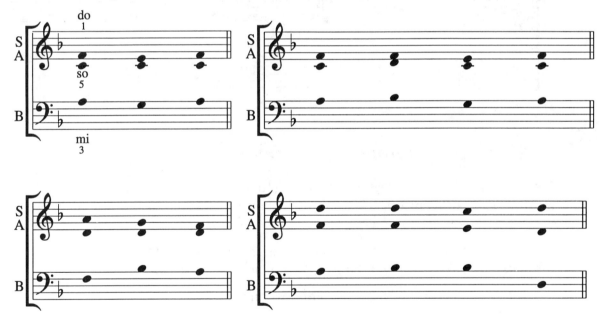

Sight-Singing

Sight-sing the exercise using solfège syllables and hand signs or numbers. Which pitch is the tonal center? Find the *mi-la* skips. Describe how the three parts work together in this exercise.

Singing: "Shalom, My Friends"

There are many different ways to work with a friend. Sometimes you both do the same job together, in unison. Sometimes you may do one part of the task and have your friend do the other part.

Think about how a piece of music might demonstrate these different ways of working with a friend. How might the parts be divided for performance?

Now turn to the music for "Shalom, My Friends" on page 53.

HOW DID YOU DO?

?

You and your friends worked together to perform "Shalom, My Friends."
1. Describe how the parts worked together at different points in the piece.
2. Can you sing from the beginning to measure 13 with two friends—each one from another section of the choir?

3. Describe what it means when a melody is minor rather than major. Do you like this sound? Why? Why not?

Shalom, My Friends

Traditional
Douglas E. Wagner
Based on a traditional Hebrew melody

Three-part Mixed Chorus and Piano

Reproduced by permission. Permit # 275772.

lom.   Sha - lom, my friends, sha - lom, my friends, sha -

lom,   sha - lom.   Sha - lom, my friends, sha -

lom.   Sha - lom,   sha - lom,   sha -

lom,   sha - lom,   sha - lom.   Sha - lom,

lom, my friends, sha - lom,   sha - lom.   Sha - lom,   sha -

lom,   sha - lom,   sha - lom.   Sha - lom,   sha -

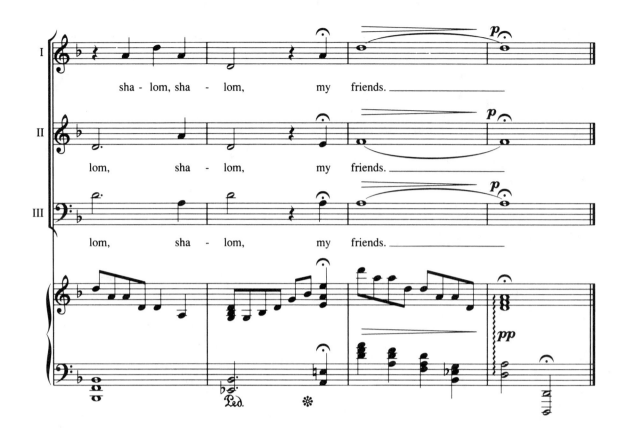

sha - lom, sha - lom,   my   friends. _____

lom,   sha - lom,   my   friends. _____

lom,   sha - lom,   my   friends. _____

LESSON 7

Whisper! Whisper!

COMPOSER: *Jay Althouse*
TEXT: *Jay Althouse*

CHORAL MUSIC TERMS

block chords

broken chord

solo and response

tonic chord

VOICING

Three-part mixed

PERFORMANCE STYLE

Spirited

A cappella

FOCUS

• Distinguish between broken and block versions of the tonic chord.

• Perform call-and-response segments of a choral piece.

Warming Up

Vocal Warm-Up

Read these examples with solfège syllables and hand signs. Where do you hear and see the broken tonic chord? Where do you hear and see scalewise motion?

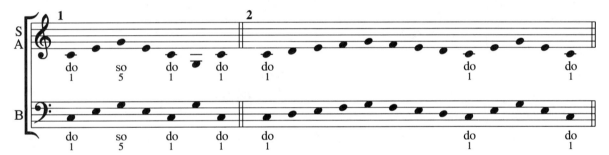

Rhythm Drill

Choose one line or the other and sight-read these rhythms. Clap each line alone, then combine them. How do the parts relate to one another? How would you make this a call and response?

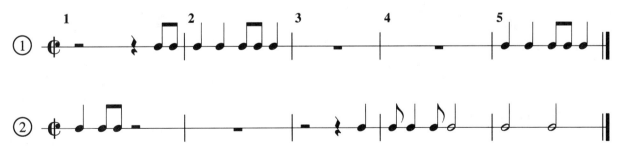

Sight-Singing

Sight-sing these chords using solfège syllables and hand signs or numbers. The tonic chord includes the syllables *do*, *mi*, and *so*. Can you find which chords in this example are tonic chords?

Singing: "Whisper! Whisper!"

Do you know any school cheers? Have someone lead the class in a cheer! Next, try the same cheer, but whisper the words. Compare how you felt performing it both ways.

Now turn to the music for "Whisper! Whisper!" on page 61.

HOW DID YOU DO?

? ?

Sometimes sections of a choir take turns being the leader, and sometimes they all work together. Sometimes pitches of a chord take turns, being heard one after the other, and sometimes they are all heard at once. Think about your activities with "Whisper! Whisper!" and answer these questions:

1. What have you learned about chords during this lesson?
2. Are you better at reading rhythms or pitches?
3. Can you and two friends from other sections of the choir demonstrate a tonic chord, both broken and as a block chord?

Whisper! Whisper!

Words and Music by
JAY ALTHOUSE

Three-part Mixed Voices, A cappella*

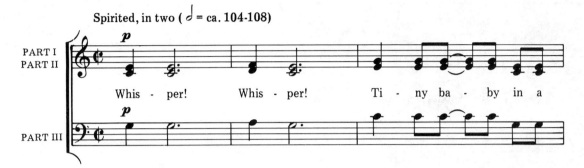

* Also available for S.A.T.B. voices (5796)

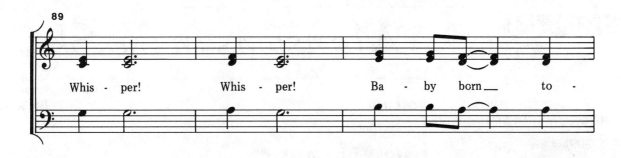

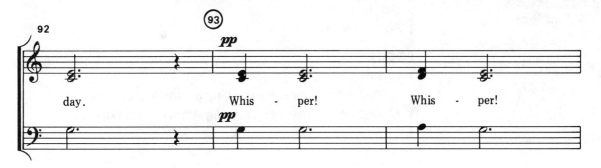

LESSON 8

Mansions in the Sky

COMPOSER: *Carl Strommen*
TEXT: *Carl Strommen*

CHORAL MUSIC TERMS
a tempo
mezzo forte (mf)
mezzo piano (mp)

VOICING
Three-part mixed

PERFORMANCE STYLE
Gently
Accompanied by piano

FOCUS
- Read and sing in three parts.
- Distinguish between and sing unison and chords.
- Distinguish between and sing stepwise and skipwise melodic motion.

Warming Up

Vocal Warm-Up
Sing these chords using solfège. Notice the pitches where all three parts are in unison, and those that have different chord tones.

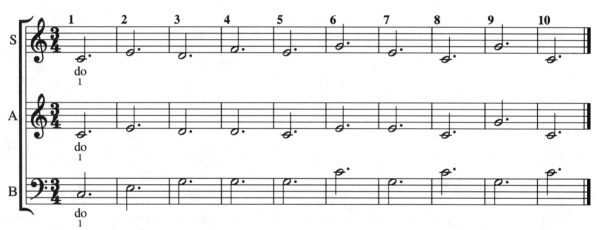

Sight-Singing

Read and sing this exercise using solfège. Where does each melody move in steps or skips? Which is easier to sing?

Singing: "Mansions in the Sky"

People say your wishes and dreams are like mansions in the sky.

When you dream, you help build your mansion.
When you wish, your mind imagines your mansion.
When you work hard, you move closer to achieving your dreams.

Read the text of "Mansions in the Sky." What does the little bird represent?

Now turn to the music for "Mansions in the Sky" on page 70.

HOW DID YOU DO?

? ?

If you set your sights on learning a new piece and work hard, you should see positive results.

Think about your preparation and performance of "Mansions in the Sky."
1. What was easy about reading the music of "Mansions in the Sky"? What was hard?
2. Describe the difference between stepwise and skipwise melodic movement. How can this help you read music?

3. Describe the difference between unison and chord tone singing. Which is easier? Which do you like better?
4. How well did you perform "Mansions in the Sky"? How well did the choir do? What criteria did you use to make this evaluation?

Lesson 8: Mansions in the Sky **69**

Mansions in the Sky

Words and Music by
CARL STROMMEN

Three-part Mixed Voices and Piano*

* Also available for S.A.T.B. (5770) and S.S.A./2-part voices (5772).

man - sions in the sky._____ Swift - ly

man - sions in the sky._____ Swift - ly

man - sions in the sky._____ Swift - ly

now, a - way the morn - ing is nigh, to

now, a - way the morn - ing is nigh,____ to

now, a - way the morn - ing is nigh, to____

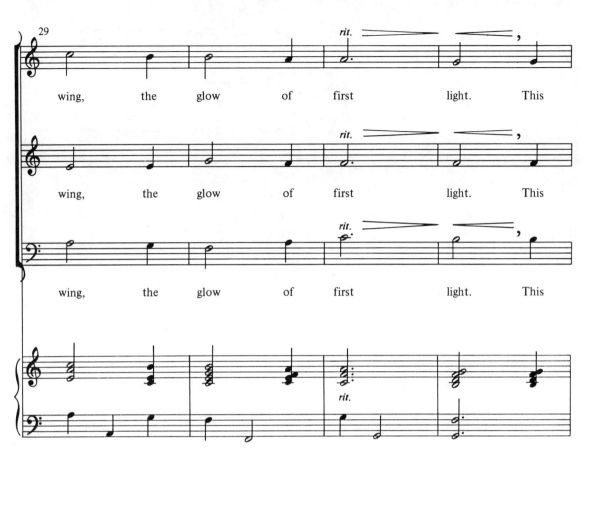

wing,   the   glow   of   first   light.   This

wing,   the   glow   of   first   light.   This

wing,   the   glow   of   first   light.   This

shin - ing hour, this break of day, to

shin - ing hour, this break of day, to

shin - ing hour, this break of day, to

man - sions in the sky._____ Lit - tle

man - sions in the sky._____ Lit - tle

man - sions in the sky._____ Lit - tle

With strength

bird, fly a - way to a dis - tant land. Lit - tle

bird, fly a - way to a dis - tant land. Lit - tle

bird, fly a - way to a dis - tant land.___ Lit - tle

LESSON 9

Down by the Riverside

Traditional, Spiritual
ARRANGER: Brad Printz

CHORAL MUSIC TERMS

key change

part independence

syncopation

VOICING

Three-part mixed

PERFORMANCE STYLE

Spiritual

Accompanied by piano

FOCUS

- Read and clap syncopated rhythms.
- Sing in two parts with independent melody and rhythm lines.

Warming Up

Rhythm Drill

Clap the following exercise. After you feel secure, clap the three parts together. There's syncopation in the Rhythm Drill, and syncopation makes the rhythm swing.

Can you find three places where there is syncopation?

Vocal Warm-up

Use the tonic triad—*do, mi, so*—in the key of G major to sing the Rhythm Drill. Use *do* for Line 1, *so* for Line 2, and *mi* for Line 3. Sing each line separately, then all together.

Now try using scat syllables to make these rhythms swing! Use any combination of these sounds: *dah, dah-bah, shoo, boop,* etc. Just make it up as you go along. Working in a group, make up your own scat pattern using the best ideas of group members.

Sight-Singing

Sight-sing these parts using solfège syllables or numbers. These two parts have melodies in contrasting motion. Look at the parts and decide how you can tell when there is contrasting motion.

Singing: "Down by the Riverside"

Change is important in music, and in life. When changes are made, we have to adjust. In "Over There" (Lesson 3), there are several key changes.

Explain what a key change is in your own words.

How might a key change affect a piece of music for the singer? For the listener? What other changes might a composer make in a piece of music?

Now turn to the music for "Down by the Riverside" on page 79.

Now turn to the music for "Down by the Riverside" on page 79.

HOW DID YOU DO?

Think about your performance of the Rhythm Drill, Sight-Singing, and "Down by the Riverside."

1. How well did you perform the syncopated rhythms?

2. How well are you sight-singing? With what do you need help?

3. Can you sing measures 73–78 with just a trio—one student performing each part? Choose another short segment of "Down by the Riverside," and perform it as a trio.

4. The song "Down by the Riverside" is about a change from war to a world of peace. How do you feel about this message?

Down by the Riverside

Traditional, Spiritual
BRAD PRINTZ

Three-part Mixed Chorus and Piano*

Duration: approx. 2:45
*Also available for Two-part (15/1012).

Special TRAK-PAK 16 (99/1027) also available.

Reproduced by permission. Permit # 275772.

LESSON 10

Something Told the Wild Geese

CHORAL MUSIC TERMS
cadence
chords
composer
mood
phrase
3/4 meter
tuning

COMPOSER: *Sherri Porterfield*
TEXT: *Rachel Field* (1894–1942)

VOICING
Three-part mixed

PERFORMANCE STYLE
With anticipated motion
Accompanied by piano

FOCUS
- Perform correctly shaped musical phrases.
- Demonstrate good intonation while singing with two other parts.

Warming Up

Rhythm Drill

In music, a phrase is a complete thought. How can you clap the A section below so it feels like a phrase? Clap each line keeping a steady 3/4 beat. Then together as a group clap the A section, and divide into three parts for the B section. Try the Rhythm Drill this way: A, BI, A, BI and BII, A, BI and BII and BIII, A. Do you feel each phrase acts as a complete thought?

Vocal Warm-Up

Sing the following chords, using solfège and hand signs. Listen to each chord and tune it before moving to the next. One sharp in the key signature could mean G major or E minor. Are these examples in G or E? How do you know?

Sight-Singing

Sight-sing these parts using solfège syllables or numbers. Where are there chords? Tune the chords carefully as you sing. Practice shaping the phrases.

Singing: "Something Told the Wild Geese"

When geese begin flying south, it's a sign that summer is over, and winter is near. What mood might you feel as you see the geese flying? When the geese fly, each individual becomes part of a larger group. Compare this to when you sing, you add your individual voice to the group.

Listen to "Something Told the Wild Geese." What mood did the composer convey? Was it similar to your mood? How did the composer convey her imagined mood?

Now turn to the music for "Something Told the Wild Geese" on page 93.

HOW DID YOU DO?

Think about your preparation and performance of "Something Told the Wild Geese." Compare your individual performance with that of the whole ensemble.

1. What did you do well by yourself? How did the group do?

2. Where do you need more work? Where does the group need more work?
3. Did you work together to build phrases? What did you do?
4. How did you enhance the mood of the piece through your performance?

Something Told the Wild Geese

Sherri Porterfield
Rachel Field (Used by Permission)

Three-part Mixed Chorus

Duration: approx. 2:00

Special TRAK-PAK 16 (99/1027) also available.

*Also available for Two-part (H5890).

stiff - ened   at re-mem - bered   ice.____

at re-mem - bered   ice.

Some-thing told   the   wild   geese   it was time   to

LESSON 11

Praise Ye the Lord, All Nations

CHORAL MUSIC TERMS

allegro

cantata

COMPOSER: *Johann S. Bach (1685–1750)*
ARRANGER: *Arnold B. Sherman*

VOICING

SAB

PERFORMANCE STYLE

Allegro
Accompanied by keyboard

FOCUS

- Sing your part independently with the other voice parts.
- Read notation in 3/4 meter including half, quarter, and eighth notes.

Warming Up

Vocal Warm-Up

Sing these parts using solfège. Describe the musical features of this Vocal Warm-Up including as many of the following as possible: rhythms, meter, key, and melodic and structural features.

Sight-Singing

Sight-sing the following exercise on *loo*. Work toward singing the entire phrase using only one breath. Be sure not to strain your voice. Sizzle the rhythms, using a *tss* sound, to make them accurate and crisp. Now try singing the exercise using different vowels, for example: *na, ne, ni, no,* and *nu.* Use the long, pure vowel sounds, like the vowels are saying their own names.

Singing: "Praise Ye the Lord, All Nations"

Sometimes a performance captivates an audience, regardless of the type of music being sung or played.

What are some reasons an audience might become captivated by the music? What are the musical elements that make a performance appealing?

Now turn to and perform the music for "Praise Ye the Lord, All Nations" on page 100.

HOW DID YOU DO?

? ?

A strong choir needs to perform as a team comprising strong, independent players who work together toward a common goal.
1. Are you a strong, independent singer? How do you know?
2. Were you able to sight-sing "Praise Ye the Lord, All Nations"?

3. Are you a strong contributing member of the team when you perform? How do you know?
4. Was the choir able to sight-sing "Praise Ye the Lord, All Nations"?
5. What did you practice to make your performance better?

Praise Ye the Lord, All Nations

Psalm 117, Adapted by A.B.S.
Johann S. Bach
Arranged by Arnold B. Sherman

SAB Chorus with Keyboard Accompaniment

Bass line may be supported by appropriate bass instrument (Cello, Bassoon, etc.).

Lord,___ all_ na - tions! Praise_____ Him,

Praise ye the Lord,___ all_ na - tions! Praise_____

Praise_____ Him.

_____ Him.

(accompaniment begins here)

Great is his

peo - ples on earth. Ex - tol him, ex - tol him, all peo - ples on

earth.   Ex - tol him, ex - tol him, all

peo - ples on earth! Ex - tol him, all peo - ples on earth!

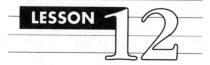

Wiegenlied

COMPOSER: *Johannes Brahms* (1833–1897)
ARRANGER: *Sherri Porterfield*
ENGLISH TEXT: *Sherri Porterfield*

CHORAL MUSIC TERMS

chord building

dynamics

I, IV, and V chords

phrase

VOICING

Three-part mixed

PERFORMANCE STYLE

With tenderness
Accompanied by piano

FOCUS

- Sing, demonstrating an understanding of phrase.
- Use correct German pronunciation for the song text.
- Build I, IV, and V chords in the key of E♭ major.

Warming Up

Rhythm Drill

Clap the phrases of rhythm softly, shaping each phrase so it sounds like part of a story you are telling with your hands. Notice the dynamic markings (< >) and the breath (ʼ) mark. Where does the second phrase start? How do you know? Compare the two phrases. How are they the same? How are they different? Divide your class into two groups. Have Group 1 clap phrase 1 as a question; have Group 2 clap phrase 2 as an answer.

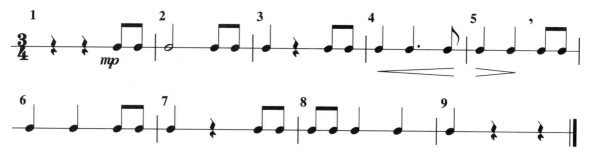

Vocal Warm-Up

Sight-sing using solfège syllables and hand signs or numbers. Repeat each exercise one step higher or lower on each repetition.

Sight-Singing

Sight-sing these examples using solfège and hand signs. Add the German text, focusing on vowel sounds. Notice that a chord is built in each second measure.

Singing: "Wiegenlied"

Have you ever heard or watched adults try to put babies to sleep? How do they move? What do they say? Do they sing? What are the characteristics of the music, language, or movement you would use to get a baby to go to sleep?

Now turn to the music for "Wiegenlied" on page 107.

Read the new translation of the German text. Do you think these words would soothe a crying baby or small child? Why?

HOW DID YOU DO?

? ?

"Wiegenlied" is one of the most famous and loved lullabies in Western music.
1. What characteristics of "Wiegenlied" do you think make it so valued?
2. Was your performance of "Wiegenlied" a convincing lullaby? How do you know?
3. Discuss how phrase is important in "Wiegenlied," and how you used the idea of phrase in your planning of the performance of the piece.

4. How difficult or easy was it to sing in German?
5. Can you point to examples of I, IV, and V chords in E♭ in "Wiegenlied"? Can you write examples of these chords?

Wiegenlied

COMPOSER: *Johannes Brahms*
ARRANGER: *Sherri Porterfield*
ENGLISH TEXT: *Sherri Porterfield*

Three-part Mixed, Accompanied

dacht___ mit Näg - lein be - steckt,
schlüpf_ un - ter die

ros - es to___ keep you safe and warm
to___ shield you from all

Deck`: Mor-gen früh, wenn Gott will, wirst du wie - der ge -

harm. Ear - ly morn soon shall come; God will wake you with

weckt, Mor-gen früh, wenn Gott will, wirst du wie - der ge -

sun, Ear - ly morn soon shall come; God will wake you with

Traum's Pa - ra - dies!
hold par - a - dise!

Schlaf' nun se - lig und süss,
Close your eyes my sweet child

schau' im
and be-

rit.   *a tempo*

Traum's Pa - ra - dies!
hold par - a - dise!

Gu - ten A - bend, gut'
Go to sleep, lit - tle

Nacht,
one,

gut' Nacht.
good night.

gut' Nacht._____
good night._____

p

rit. **pp**

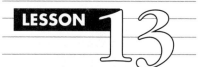

LESSON 13

Nightfall

COMPOSER: *Lou Williams-Wimberly*
TEXT: *Henry Wadsworth Longfellow (1807–1882)*

CHORAL MUSIC TERMS
breathing mechanics
staccato
legato

VOICING
SAB

PERFORMANCE STYLE
Slow
A cappella

FOCUS
- Describe and demonstrate correct breathing mechanics.
- Describe and demonstrate legato singing style.

Warming Up

 Vocal Warm-Up

Sing this exercise using solfège syllables or numbers. Listen carefully and tune to the group. Each note is related to the ones beside it, and to others in the phrase. Sing the exercise with separated, staccato tones. Be sure to keep in tune. Sing the exercise again with legato, attached tones.

Sight-Singing

Sight-sing the parts below using solfège syllables or numbers. What are the characteristics of "good breathing"? Use them when you sing this exercise. Decide where you might take a breath in this piece. Try several places. Can you sing it all on one breath without straining your voice?

Singing: "Nightfall"

Imagine a feather on your hand. Blow it gently up into the air, and watch its imaginary path. Describe the path your imaginary feather took. Compare that path to the "rise and fall" of musical phrases.

Now turn to the music for "Nightfall" on page 113.

HOW DID YOU DO?

Think about your performance of "Nightfall."
1. Can you sight-sing the pitches and rhythms? When do you feel most confident?
2. Describe the mechanics of good breathing, then sing a phrase to demonstrate your ability.

3. Describe legato singing, and sing a phrase to demonstrate your description.
4. What musical tools did the composer use to convey the feeling of "Nightfall"?

Nightfall

Lou Williams-Wimberly
Henry Wadsworth Longfellow

down - ward from an ea - gle in his flight.

down - ward from an ea - gle in his flight.

down - ward from an ea - gle in his flight.

comes o'er me That my soul can - not re - sist. Come, read to me some

comes o'er me That my soul can - not re - sist. Come, read to me some

comes o'er me That my soul can - not re - sist. Come, read to me some

SC 360

poem, Some sim - ple heart - felt lay, That shall soothe this rest - less

poem, Some sim - ple heart - felt lay, That shall soothe this rest - less

poem, Some sim - ple heart - felt lay, That shall soothe this rest - less

feel - ing And ban - ish the thoughts of day. And then the

feel - ing And ban - ish the thoughts of day. And then the

feel - ing And ban - ish the thoughts of day. And then the

SC 360

night shall be filled with mu-sic That will qui-et my ev-'ry care, And

night shall be filled with mu-sic That will qui-et my ev-'ry care, And

night shall be filled with mu-sic That will qui-et my ev-'ry care, And

come like the ben-e-dic-tion That fol-lows af-ter pray'r.

come like the ben-e-dic-tion That fol-lows af-ter pray'r.

come like the ben-e-dic-tion That fol-lows af-ter pray'r.

SC 360

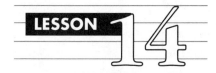
Riu, Riu, Chiu

Anonymous Spanish Carol (1556)
ARRANGER: *Linda Steen Spevacek*
ENGLISH TEXT: *Linda Steen Spevacek*

CHORAL MUSIC TERMS

doubling
F minor
la tonal center
meter changes
3/2 meter

VOICING

SAB

PERFORMANCE STYLE

Rhythmically, with a lilt
A cappella
Optional: Tambourine and Hand Claps

FOCUS

- Read in F minor, using solfège syllables and hand signs or numbers.
- Perform correct meter changes from 2/2 to 3/2 and back.
- Use correct Spanish pronunciation.

Warming Up

 Vocal Warm-Up

Sing these chord drills on *loo* to become familiar with the key of F minor. Is *do* or *la* the tonal center of each exercise below? How do you know?

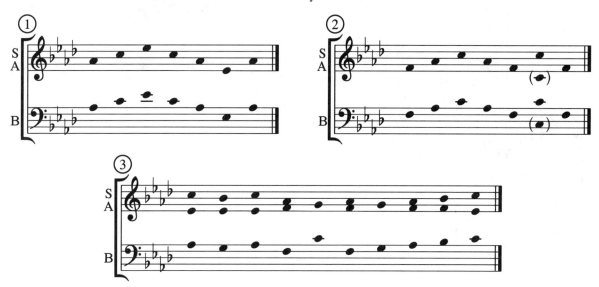

 Rhythm Drill

Clap the following exercise. Notice the time change. What type of note gets one beat in 2/2 meter? Have a beat keeper play on every beat. When you get to 3/2 meter, there will be an extra beat in each measure. In 2/2 meter, every other beat is strong. In 3/2 meter every third beat is strong.

Sight-Singing

Sight-sing the parts below using solfège syllables or numbers. Sometimes pitches are doubled in a chord. Then you might only hear two pitches. Name the chords that are suggested on the first beat of each measure. What mood or feeling does this doubling give?

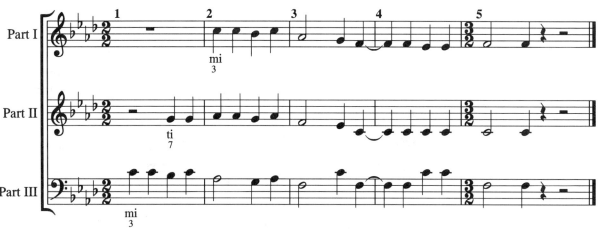

Singing: "Riu, Riu, Chiu"

Sometimes musical interest is created by change. Sometimes it can be created through repetition. Look at the three exercises you have read, and predict what types of changes you might expect in "Riu, Riu, Chiu." Listen to "Riu, Riu, Chiu" and tell how musical interest is maintained. Now turn to the music for "Riu, Riu, Chiu" on page 119.

HOW DID YOU DO?

"Riu, Riu, Chiu" has lots of repetition.
1. Tell how you kept the piece interesting.
2. Explain how the meter changes from 2/2 to 3/2 works, using the words *beat* and *strong beats*. Then sing measures 1–8 to demonstrate your understanding.
3. What is the tonal center of this piece? Choose and sing a phrase in solfège that shows the tonal center.

4. How was your Spanish pronunciation?
5. Tape record the group performing "Riu, Riu, Chiu," then write a critique describing what you heard. Tell what you liked and what could be improved.

Ríu, Ríu, Chíu

Anonymous Spanish Carol (1556)
Arranged by Linda Steen Spevacek
Original English text by L.S.S.

Three-part Mixed Chorus, A cappella,
and Optional Tambourine, Hand Claps, and Spanish text

Duration: approx. 1:50

*Transpose to any key, depending on the tessitura and time of year.

**Ríu, ríu, chíu is the call (or sounds) of the nightingale. The English is not intended as a translation. Rather, it is a
new, secular text that adapts for more general use. The Spanish text is sacred and may be sung when appropriate.

Included on Trak-Pak 21 (99/1060H)

wait - ing in the wing.   When you find it, come, come and join him now and

es - tra vo - lun - tad,   pues a se i - gua - lar con el hom - bre vi -

Clap: (All Parts)

sing, __   "Rí - u, rí - u, chí - u," hear __ the joy - ful sing - ing,

nie - ra.   "Rí - u, rí - u, chí - u," la __ guar - da ri - be - ra:

sing. __   "Rí - u, rí - u, chí - u," hear __ the joy - ful sing - ing,

nie - ra.   "Rí - u, rí - u, chí - u," la __ guar - da ri - be - ra:

"Rí - u, rí - u, chí - u," hear __ the joy - ful sing - ing,

"Rí - u, rí - u, chí - u," la __ guar - da ri - be - ra:

Tambourine:

Making Historical Connections

The *Madonna and Child* by Giovanni Bellini (c. 1430–1516) expresses a calm and idyllic mood. This mood is similar to the quiet, devotional quality of Renaissance religious music.

c. 1470–75. Giovanni Bellini. *Madonna and Child*. Tempera and oil on wood panel. 82 x 58 cm (32⅜ x 22¾"). Kimbell Art Museum, Fort Worth, Texas.

Renaissance Period

COMPOSERS

Guillaume Dufay (1400–1474)
Josquin Desprez (c. 1440–1521)
William Cornysh (c. 1465–1523)
Christopher Tye (c. 1500–c. 1572)
Giovanni Pierluigi da Palestrina
   (c. 1525–1594)
Orlande de Lassus (1532–1594)
Luca Marenzio (1553–1599)
Michael Praetorius (c. 1571–1621)
Thomas Weelkes (1575–1623)

ARTISTS

Donatello (1386–1466)
Giovanni Bellini (c. 1430–1516)
Leonardo da Vinci (1452–1519)
Michelangelo (1475–1564)
Raphael (1483–1520)
Titian (c. 1488–1576)

AUTHORS

Martin Luther (1483–1546)
Sir Walter Raleigh (c. 1552–1618)
Sir Philip Sidney (1554–1586)
William Shakespeare (1564–1616)

After completing this lesson, you will be able to:

- *Describe the developments that took place in music during the Renaissance period.*
- *Compare the differences in sacred music between the Middle Ages and the Renaissance.*
- *Define* madrigal, Renaissance, *and* polyphony.

Think of recent discoveries that have changed your life. Due to advances in technology and communications, you are living in a time of great change. Sophisticated computers and telecommunications systems affect how you receive and process information. Explorers are traveling into space and deep into the ocean. New scientific discoveries are making life better on Earth, and better *for* Earth. New art and music styles are being created. Some people say that we live in a very exciting time, because we are only now realizing the range of possibilities before us.

The Renaissance—a Time of Rebirth

The fifteenth and sixteenth centuries were a similar time in history. This period has become known as the **Renaissance,** which means *rebirth* or *renewal*. During the Renaissance period (c. 1430–1600), tremendous growth and discoveries took place. Great achievements occurred in music, art, and literature.

At the same time, explorers traveled to new continents and experienced very different cultures. Scientists such as Copernicus, Galileo, and da Vinci explored the idea that the Earth was not the center of everything, but perhaps revolved around the sun. In the early 1500s, the Protestant Reformation, led by Martin Luther, began and brought about other important developments in religion, politics, and music.

One of the most important contributions of the Renaissance, however, is attributed to Johann Gutenberg, who perfected the printing press in the mid-1400s. The invention of movable type accelerated opportunities to learn. Before that time, books were rare and expensive and had to be copied by hand. With the printing press came mass-produced books, and many more people were able to learn the arts of reading both words and music.

Looking Back

Most written music during the Middle Ages (eleventh to the fifteenth centuries) was composed for and performed in church. Many of the texts were taken mainly from the Book of Psalms

CHORAL MUSIC TERMS
madrigal
polyphony
Renaissance
sacred music
secular music

Gutenberg press;
beginning of modern printing

▼ c. 1435

Sistine Chapel construction begins

▼ 1473

Columbus lands in
West Indies/Americas

▼ 1492

▲ 1465

First printed music appears

▲ 1480

Sistine Chapel finished

in the Old Testament of the Bible. The music was chanted in unison in Latin, without accompaniment. This musical form is called Gregorian chant, and it marks the beginning of Western art music. Many of these chants, as well as popular folk melodies, became the basis for two-, three-, or four-part compositions. Since the voices used were of equal ranges and vocal quality, the sound of vocal groups during the Middle Ages lacked a full choral range. During the Middle Ages, however, scales, solfège, and the beginnings of musical notation were developed.

▲ **The artists and architects of the Renaissance rediscovered classical antiquity and were inspired by what they found. In 1547, Michelangelo (1475–1564) became chief architect for the replacement of the original basilica of Old St. Peter's. Architect Giacomo della Porta finished the dome 26 years after Michelangelo's death.**

1546–64. Michelangelo. Exterior view, St. Peter's. St. Peter's Basilica, Vatican State, Rome, Italy. (Dome completed by Giacomo della Porta, 1590.)

Music and Art

The Renaissance was a time when scholars and artists became interested in the study of Greek and Roman art, architecture, and philosophy. The major artists of the period, such as Leonardo da Vinci, Raphael, Titian, Michelangelo, Bellini, and Donatello began to capture the new feeling of individuality and human achievement that was emerging. You will notice that their art celebrates the lifelike and realistic appearance of the individual.

New art and music styles emerged. **Sacred music,** or *hymns, chorales,* and *early masses,* also changed. Eventually, the equal-voice quality of the music of the Middle Ages developed into the full choral range of the present-day choir.

Imitative forms continued to develop, with more and more independence of parts. Now the music could be printed, distributed, and read. Instruments such as organs, strings (lute and viol), and winds (recorder, shawm) began to be used with voices in processions and other ceremonies. Martin Luther believed that languages other than Latin were suitable for worship, so he translated the Bible into German. He then composed hymns in German so everyone could sing parts

Magellan begins voyage around the world

1519

Composer William Byrd born

1543

1517

Protestant Reformation begins in Germany with Luther's 95 Theses

1584

Sir Walter Raleigh discovers Virginia

1522

Magellan's crew ends voyage around the world

of the church services.

Secular music, *any music that is not sacred,* also flourished during the Renaissance. For the first time in history, musicians traveled throughout Europe, bringing new styles from one country to another. Popular songs and madrigals were common and were frequently fused to create even newer styles. A **madrigal** is *a secular vocal form written in several imitative parts.* Each part is equally important, and the parts weave together to form polyphony. **Polyphony** means that *each voice part begins at a different place, is independent and important, and sections often repeat in contrasting dynamic levels* (poly—many, phony—sounds).

Choral music became more and more complex. Because more people were reading and singing composed songs, the range and depth of expression expanded. While polyphony existed during the Middle Ages, it was developed during the Renaissance, causing this period to frequently be called "the golden age of polyphony." People sang polyphony in church, at home, and for celebrations.

A Modern Renaissance

You also live in an age of great change, combined with tremendous possibilities. This time could be compared to that of the Renaissance. Perhaps your creativity and imagination will inspire you to be one of the new explorers, inventors, artists, or musicians who will discover new ways to look at the world.

Check Your Understanding

Recall

1. Describe some of the nonmusical changes that occurred during the Renaissance.

2. How did sacred music change from the Middle Ages to the Renaissance?

3. How did secular music change during the Renaissance?

4. Define a madrigal.

5. Describe polyphony.

Thinking It Through

1. Compare the influence of the printing press during the Renaissance to the development of the computer today. What modern changes are similar to the changes that occurred during the Renaissance?

2. What new skills did people need to learn in order to participate in music during the Renaissance?

Listening to . . .
Renaissance Music

CHORAL SELECTION

Marenzio — "Cantate Ninfe"

Luca Marenzio (1553–1599) composed "Cantate Ninfe," a light and airy piece that is a worthy representative of Renaissance music. In this composition, Marenzio's use of "text painting" coupled with independent parts moving to chords and cadences create a texture typical of Renaissance music. "Cantate Ninfe" provides a reliable example of music that comes from the period in history in which Europe transitioned from the Middle Ages to more modern classical and humanistic concepts.

INSTRUMENTAL SELECTION

Anonymous — "Saltarello"

The word *saltarello* is a broad term for swift Italian folk dances. These dances involve jumping and are usually in triple meter. Generally, a saltarello consists of several repeated melodies with each melody having a different ending. The origin of these dances is unknown, but the earliest recorded use of saltarello as a musical term is in the late fourteenth and early fifteenth centuries. Saltarellos were popular throughout several different musical periods because of their authentic folk-dance quality.

Introducing...

"Kyrie Eleison"

Antonio Lotti

Setting the Stage

Translated to mean "Lord, have mercy upon us," the "Kyrie Eleison" is customarily the first prayer of the Ordinary of the Mass. It is suitable for both church and concert use. Its polyphonic textures and imitative melodies are a perfect example of Renaissance religious music, as well as many other forms of the time. The time signature and bar lines would not have been written during this time period, therefore they are additions to the music. This rendition includes both the Greek text and the English translation. Let this piece transport you back to a time long ago.

Meeting the Composer

Antonio Lotti (c. 1667–1740)

Antonio Lotti began his musical career as a singer in a Venetian choir and later became the lead organist. Lotti's opera career began to flourish in 1692 when his work Il Trionfo dell' Innocenza was performed in Venice. It wasn't until between 1706–1717, however, that Lotti became the most productive in composing operas, when at least 16 of his original works were staged. Lotti's works were usually composed in the style of the late Baroque period, but he also would sometimes follow the contrapuntal style of the Renaissance composer, Palestrina.

Kyrie Eleison

COMPOSER: *Antonio Lotti (c. 1667–1740)*

ARRANGER: *Dr. Lee Kjelson*

CHORAL MUSIC TERMS

contrapuntal

cut-time meter (symbol)

Kyrie Eleison

Picardy third

VOICING

SATB

PERFORMANCE STYLE

Prayerfully

A cappella

FOCUS

- Sing your voice part independently.
- Identify polyphonic textures.
- Demonstrate knowledge of correct Greek pronunciation.

Warming Up

Vocal Warm-Up

Sing the following scales in unison. Sing each scale on whole notes, then half notes, then quarter notes.

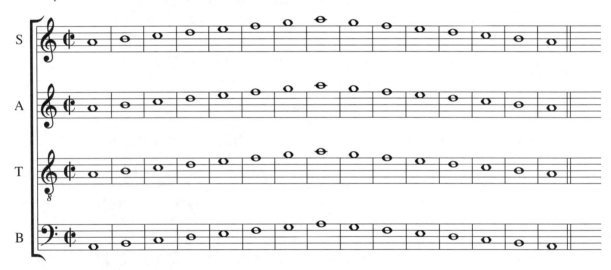

Sight-Singing

Sight-sing these parts using solfège syllables or numbers. Notice the meter signature. It tells you to sing in "cut time," or cut each note value in half. Instead of reading 4/4, you will read 2/2. Each half note gets one beat, and there are two beats in a measure. Count your rests carefully. Can you tell the difference between the parts at the beginning and end of this exercise? Where is there imitative style in this exercise? Where are there chords? What effect does the C♯ have on the last chord?

 Singing: "Kyrie Eleison"

Can you "row" in two keys?

You know how to sing rounds. Rounds are an example of imitative style. Each part imitates the one before it exactly. The overlapping parts form chords.

What happens when you sing a round in two different keys?

Sing "Row, Row, Row Your Boat" as a round in A major, then A minor. Altos and basses sing the song in D minor.

Sing it as a round: sopranos and tenors in A minor, altos and basses in D minor.

Now turn to the music for "Kyrie Eleison" on page 140.

HOW DID YOU DO? **?**	Think about your performance on the Vocal Warm-Up and "Kyrie Eleison." **1.** How does this relate to the beginning of "Kyrie Eleison"? **2.** Could you sing your part independently? **3.** Could you identify the polyphonic	textures when you heard or saw them? **4.** How was your Greek pronunciation? **5.** What characteristics of Renaissance music did you experience in this piece? **6.** Describe one thing you liked about this piece.

Kyrie Eleison

(Lord, Have Mercy Upon Us)

Antonio Lotti
Arranged by Dr. Lee Kjelson

Mixed Chorus, SATB, A cappella

RANGES:
Soprano   Alto   Tenor   Bass

From the Liturgy   Antonio Lotti

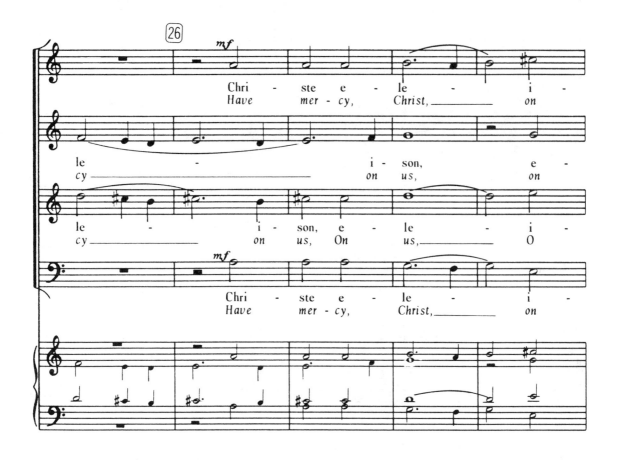

Bel.Oct.2204

▲ The dramatization observed in this sculpture, *The Ecstasy of St. Teresa* by Gianlorenzo Bernini (1598–1680), demonstrates the Baroque quest for expression and movement. Here the saint floats in space as she receives a vision of heaven. Such drama, movement, and tension are also qualities prominent in the music of the period.

1645–52. Gianlorenzo Bernini. *The Ecstasy of St. Teresa*. Marble. Life-size. Cornaro Chapel, Santa Maria della Vittoria, Rome, Italy.

Baroque Period

After completing this lesson, you will be able to:

- Describe some developments that took place during the Baroque period.
- Identify some forms and characteristics of Baroque instrumental and vocal music.
- Compare characteristics of Baroque art, architecture, and music.
- Define oratorio, cantata, and opera.

Imagine a plain, brick, rectangular building. Notice the plain door and windows. Now begin to create elaboration on the features of this building. Imagine a fancier door, decoration around the door, and ornate columns. Imagine tile work and mosaic patterns over the brick, creating a fancy exterior. Now go through the front door into the hallway to see the gold woodwork, high domed ceilings, and paintings covering the walls and ceilings. You are imagining a building from the **Baroque period** (1600–1750)—*the period of elaboration.* (**Baroque** comes from an Italian word meaning *rocky, irregular.*)

COMPOSERS

Claudio Monteverdi (1567–1643)
Arcangelo Corelli (1643–1713)
Henry Purcell (1659–1695)
Antonio Vivaldi (1678–1741)
Johann Sebastian Bach (1685–1750)
George Frideric Handel (1685–1759)

ARTISTS

El Greco (1541–1614)
Peter Paul Rubens (1577–1640)
Artemisia Gentileschi (1593–1653)
Gianlorenzo Bernini (1598–1680)
Rembrandt van Rijn (1606–1669)
Judith Leyster (1609–1660)

AUTHORS

John Donne (c.1573–1631)
Rene Descartes (1596–1650)
John Milton (1608–1674)
Molière (1622–1673)

The Baroque Period—a Time of Elaboration

The Baroque period in music developed around 1600. It reached its height and ended with the death of Johann Sebastian Bach in 1750. During this period, Baroque artists and musicians had a style that characteristically had dramatic flair and dynamic movement. The *music became so elaborate toward the end of this period (mid-1700s)* that it was termed **Rococo**.

CHORAL MUSIC TERMS

Baroque period
cantata
continuo
elaboration
improvised
opera
oratorio
Rococo

Looking Back

The Renaissance was a period of change, during which there was an increased interest and involvement in cultural activities. The invention of the printing press created a society in which reading and writing were more widely known, and ideas began to be easily shared. Sacred music was written with the increased involvement of everyday people, and secular music began to emerge with strong melody lines.

Music of the Baroque

During the Baroque period, there was a strong desire to classify and assimilate all knowledge. The strength of the individual's spirit and will shaped a very emotional sense of splendor in the arts.

Galileo	Henry Hudson explores the Hudson River	Pilgrims land in America	Isaac Newton	Quakers arrive in Massachusetts
▼ 1564–1642	▼ 1609	▼ 1620	▼ 1642–1727	▼ 1656

▲ 1607
Jamestown, Virginia
established settlement

▲ 1618–1648
Thirty Years' War

▲ 1636
Harvard College
founded

▲ 1643–1715
Reign of Louis XIV, King of France

▲ 1608
Telescope invented

The music of the Baroque period reflected the elaborate attitudes of society. Compositions had a strong sense of movement, many times with a *continually moving bass line*, called **continuo.** Melodies were highly ornamental, and more ornamentations were often **improvised,** *invented on the spur of the moment*, during performances. Underneath all the fancy elaboration, however, remained the clear, classical, mathematically precise forms and thinking symbolized by the plain, brick rectangular building you imagined earlier in the example on page 145. The sense of symmetry and planning is clear in the music of the Baroque.

Instrumental Forms

The Baroque period brought about a great interest in instrumental music. Keyboard instruments were refined and elaborated upon, including the clavichord, harpsichord, and organ. The modern string family was dominant, and the trumpet was a favorite melody instrument in the orchestras of the day.

Many new forms of music were developed during the Baroque period. The *suite* usually consisted of several movements, sometimes specific dance rhythms,

▲ **The Baroque period, the period of elaboration, is evident in the detailed exterior of the Palace at Versailles. In 1661, France's King Louis XIV ordered architects to build him the largest, most elaborate palace in the world.**

1682. Louis Le Vau and Jules Hardoin-Mansart. The Cour d'honneur of the Castle at Versailles. Chateau, Versailles, France.

Johann Sebastian Bach

1685–1750

First American newspaper
established, *Boston News Letter*

1704

Handel comes to England

1710

1682

LaSalle explores
the Mississippi

1685–1759

George Frideric Handel

1706–1790

Benjamin Franklin

1687

Publication of Newton's *Mathematical Principles*

of contrasting tempos and styles. The *concerto grosso* was a form with several movements composed for a small chamber orchestra. The concerto grosso also contrasted a small musical group with the full orchestra. The pieces featured great clarity of parts, with a moving bass line and elaborate melody.

Vocal and Mixed Forms

Opera was born during the Baroque period, and is considered one of the most important vocal developments of the time. **Opera** is *a combination of singing, instrumental music, dancing, and drama that tells a story*. It was stylized and theatrical, and had effects for their own sakes—all characteristics of Baroque art.

The **oratorio,** *a piece for solo voices, chorus, and orchestra, was an expanded dramatic work on a literary or religious theme presented without theatrical action.* One of the most famous oratorios is George Frideric Handel's *Messiah*, composed in 1741. This piece contains the famous "Hallelujah Chorus."

Another vocal form was the **cantata,** *a collection of vocal compositions with instrumental accompaniment consisting of several movements based on related secular or sacred text segments.* Movements alternated among chorus, solo, duet, and/or trio.

Baroque music is often performed today by orchestras, choirs, and smaller instrumental and vocal ensembles, both in sacred and secular settings. You might explore your community for places where Baroque music is performed.

Check Your Understanding

Recall

1. Describe some major characteristics of the Baroque period, reflected in its music and art.

2. Describe instrumental music during the Baroque period by identifying both popular instruments and some instrumental forms that were composed.

3. Identify three vocal music forms of the Baroque period.

4. Describe an oratorio, and name a famous Baroque oratorio. Who composed it?

Thinking It Through

1. Compare Renaissance and Baroque music by explaining the similarities and differences between both styles.

2. What characteristics of the Baroque period explain why people of this period enjoyed opera? Why do people in today's society still enjoy Baroque operas?

Listening to . . .

Baroque Music

CHORAL SELECTION

Bach — Cantata No. 80 "A Mighty Fortress Is Our God" No. 8

Johann Sebastian Bach (1685–1750) was a devout man of the Lutheran faith. The Lutheran hymn tunes, known as chorales, figured prominently in much of his sacred music. During his time as church organist, Bach wrote more than 140 chorales for organ. His chorale prelude on "A Mighty Fortress Is Our God," composed in 1709 in Weimar, is an extended elaboration on the tune by Martin Luther.

INSTRUMENTAL SELECTION

Bach — *Brandenburg* Concerto No. 2, First Movement

The Brandenburg Concertos were dedicated to the Margrave of Brandenburg in 1721 by Bach, who was in the service of Prince Leopold at the time. The Prince actually played in the court orchestra that Bach conducted. The *concerto grosso* was one of the prominent forms in the eighteenth century. This form revolved around the contrast between a small group of instruments and a larger group of instruments. In *Brandenburg* Concerto No. 2, the small group called a *concertino* included violin, oboe, trumpet, and recorder and the large group or *ripieno* included strings and continuo played by the cello. Sometimes the concertino played by themselves and sometimes they played with the orchestra.

Introducing...

"Alleluia"

Johann Sebastian Bach

Setting the Stage

"Alleluia" is a German chorale written as a hymn with simple rhythms and an unchanging tempo. The texture is homophonic in style and is written above a magnificently ornamented accompaniment This chorale is taken from the Christmas cantata, "For Us a Child Is Born."

Meeting the Composer

Johann Sebastian Bach (1685–1750)

Johann Sebastian Bach, the youngest of eleven children, was born in Eisenach, Germany, in 1685. He is known as one of the greatest composers in Western musical history. When he was nine years old, his parents died and Bach went to live with his brother, Johann Christoph, who was an organist. There he learned the fundamentals of keyboard with his brother and studied composition on his own until 1700.

As an organist and choirmaster for Lutheran churches near his birthplace, Bach devoted his life to composing music for the church service. He wrote wonderful music not only for the organ, but also for choral groups; for clavier and harpsichord, for orchestra, and for small groups of instruments. Bach was the master of *fugue* and he perfected the *choral-prelude*. After devoting his life to music, he died at the age of 65 in Leipzig on July 28, 1750.

As you listen to his music, you will notice the human quality that lies in Bach's music. There is a sense of passion that shines through both his text settings and his instrumental works.

BAROQUE LESSON

Alleluía

From the Christmas cantata, "*For Us a Child Is Born*"
COMPOSER: *Johann Sebastian Bach* (1685–1750)
ARRANGER: *Theron Kirk*

CHORAL MUSIC TERMS
breathing techniques
crescendo
decrescendo
dynamics
phrase

VOICING
SAB

PERFORMANCE STYLE
Allegro
Accompanied by piano

FOCUS
- Sing with proper breathing techniques.
- Define and perform dynamic markings.

Warming Up

Vocal Warm-Up

Sing the broken chords on solfège syllables in C major and A minor, holding out the chord in three parts after each broken chord. Review proper breathing techniques as shown on the handout your teacher will provide. Use them when you sing this exercise. Inhale as someone counts to 4, then sing the exercise. Decrease the number of beats allowed for breathing one beat on each repeat, until you breathe in for only one beat.

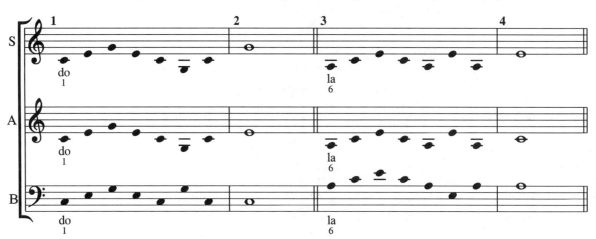

Sight-Singing

Sight-sing these parts using solfège syllables or numbers. Can you sing the whole phrase in one smooth breath? Begin *mezzo forte* and crescendo to the highest point, then decrescendo to the end. Does this change in dynamics change the feeling of the phrase for the performer? For the listener?

Singing: "Alleluia"

Elaboration means adding characteristics to make something more detailed. Think about your breathing—just plain breathing. Now think about how you must elaborate upon your breathing to sing well. Discuss the characteristics of good breathing, and how they contribute to a good vocal performance.

Now turn to the music for "Alleluia" on page 152.

HOW DID YOU DO?

?

Think about your performance on the Vocal Warm-Up and "Alleluia."
1. Could you sing your part independently?
2. Did you use proper breathing techniques?
3. How well did you follow the dynamic markings? How well did the ensemble do?

4. How was your part different from the accompaniment line?
5. What characteristics of Baroque music did you experience in this piece?
6. Describe one thing you liked about this piece.

Alleluía

From the Christmas Cantata, "For Us a Child Is Born"

Johann Sebastian Bach (1685–1750)
Arranged by Theron Kirk

Mixed Voices, SAB

Soprano

Alto

Baritone

Al -

Al -

Al -

Pro Oct 2094

le - lu - ia, Al -

le - lu - ia, Al -

le - lu - ia, Al -

le - lu - ia,

le - lu - ia,

le - lu - ia,

Give praise to our God,

Give praise to our God,

Give praise to our God,

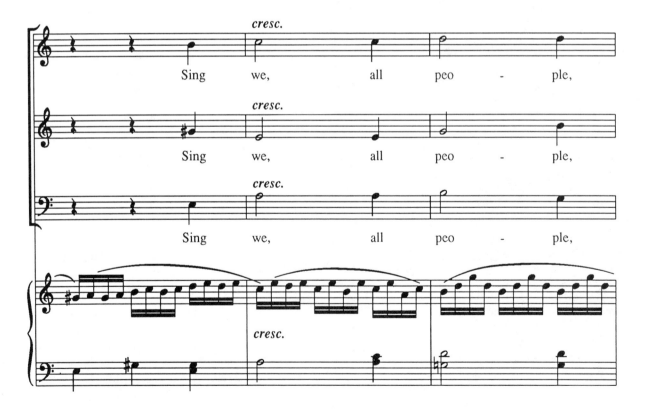

cresc.

Sing we, all peo - ple,

cresc.

Sing we, all peo - ple,

cresc.

Sing we, all peo - ple,

cresc.

Pro Oct 2094

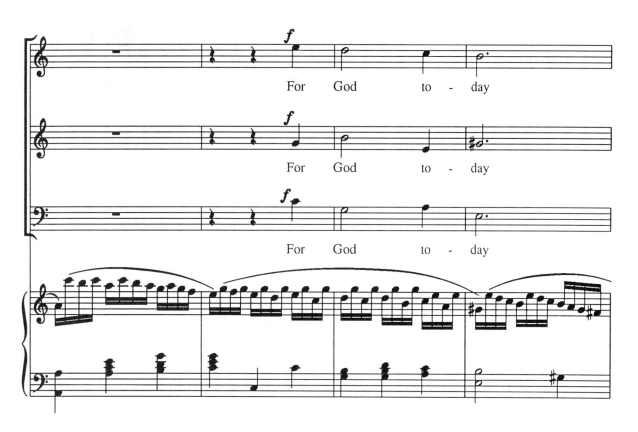

Pro Oct 2094

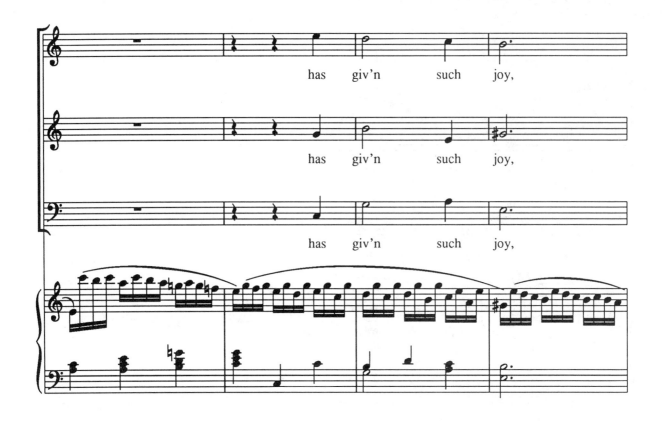

has giv'n   such   joy,

has giv'n   such   joy,

has giv'n   such   joy,

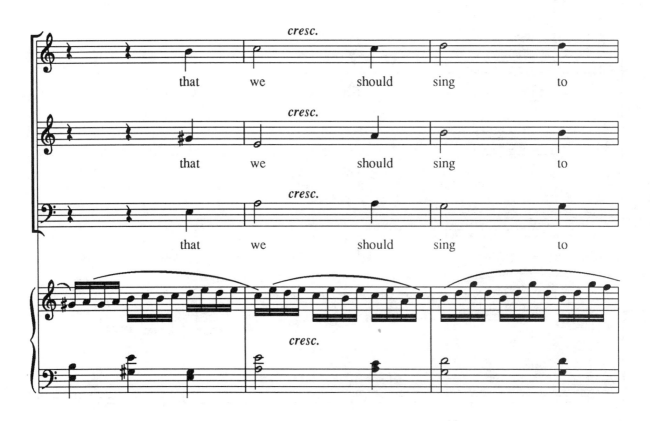

cresc.

that   we   should   sing   to

cresc.

that   we   should   sing   to

cresc.

that   we   should   sing   to

cresc.

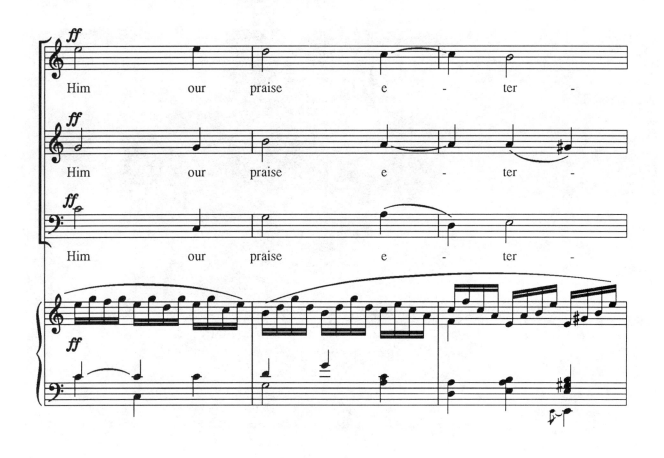

Him   our   praise   e   -   ter   -

nal.

nal.

nal.

Pro Oct 2094

The Oath of the Horatii reflects Jacques Louis David's (1748–1825) interest in the beauty of Greco-Roman subjects. This interest in idealistic Classical subjects has a parallel in the formal structures of much of the music composed during this period.

1786. Jacques Louis David. *The Oath of the Horatii.* (Detail.) Oil on canvas. 3.35 x 4.27 m (11 x 14'). Toledo Museum of Art, Toledo, Ohio.

Classical Period

After completing this lesson, you will be able to:

- Compare qualities of music written in the Classical and Baroque styles.
- Identify two major composers from the Classical period.
- Define sonata-allegro form.

Today, we have a fascination with the old. We are excited to climb pyramids or see the ruins of ancient civilizations. We glorify stories that contain archeological subjects. The **Classical period** (1750–1820) was *a time when society began looking to the ancient Greeks and Romans for examples of order and ways of looking at life.*

The Classical Period—a Time of Balance, Clarity, and Simplicity

Baroque music was written with an emotional quality that was rather flamboyant. Embellishments and virtuosity dominated compositions. In comparison, music of the Classical period gave the expression of emotion a more restrained quality. Clarity, repose, and balance took an upper hand in expressing emotion in Classical music.

In the eighteenth century, painters, sculptors, and architects took notice of the ancient Greek and Roman artifacts being excavated in Athens, Pompeii, and other archeological sites. The calmness and simplicity of this ancient, "classical" art inspired logic, symmetry, and balance and guided artists away from the overly decorative, exaggerated ideals of the Baroque.

COMPOSERS

Franz Joseph Haydn (1732–1809)
Wolfgang Amadeus Mozart (1756–1791)
Ludwig van Beethoven (1770–1827)
Vincento Bellini (1801–1835)

ARTISTS

Francois Boucher (1703–1770)
Jean-Honoré Fragonard (1732–1806)
Francisco Gôya (1746–1828)
Jacques Louis David (1748–1825)

AUTHORS

Voltaire (1694–1778)
Wolfgang Goethe (1749–1832)
Jane Austen (1775–1817)

CHORAL MUSIC TERMS
Classical period
sonata-allegro form

▲ **The Classical period reflects the renewal of interest once again in the design elements of balance, symmetry, and simplicity of line. Commissioned by Napoleon, the Arc de Triomphe du Carrousel was inspired by the Arch of Septimus Severus in Rome.**

1806. Charles Percier and Pierre F. L. Fontaine. The Arc de Triomphe in the Place du Carrousel. Arc de Triomphe du Carrousel, Paris, France.

Swift writes
Gulliver's Travels

▼ 1726

George Washington

▼ 1732–1799

Thomas Jefferson

▼ 1743–1826

● ●

▲ 1732–1757

Franklin writes *Poor Richard's Almanac*

Music of the Classical Period

During the Classical period, people developed an interest in knowing more about the cultural aspects of life, such as art and music, that had once been attainable only by the wealthy. More books were published for learning about music. Musical scores were also more widely available. Musicians, mainly supported by the wealthy and aristocratic, now wrote music that was accessible to the general public.

The two main composers associated with this period are Franz Joseph Haydn (1732–1809) and Wolfgang Amadeus Mozart (1756–1791). The large quantity and variety of their work and their faithfulness to the Classical style overshadowed many other composers of the time. Ludwig van Beethoven was born in 1770 and began composing in this period, but his work bridges the gap between the Classical and Romantic periods, the latter of which will be discussed later.

The idea of improvisation and exaggerated use of embellishments of the Baroque were abandoned for a more precise and balanced style in the Classical period. A balance between content of the music and the form in which it was expressed became an essential characteristic of the period.

Symphonies, sonatas, concertos, and chamber works became important vehicles in instrumental works. During this time, the **sonata-allegro form,** *a movement written in* A B A *form*, was born. In this form, there is a section, the *Exposition*, which represents the theme (A). The theme is then repeated with elaboration (A'). Many times this elaboration was improvised by the performer on the spot, and was a sign of his or her musical skills. The next section of the piece, the *Development*, was a contrasting section (B). Finally, there was a return to the original theme (A) in a section called *Recapitulation*.

Opera experienced a great reformation in the eighteenth century. Composers felt a need to remove its excess vocal acrobatics and to emphasize its drama.

Classical Music Today

You can hear Classical music performed in many places today. A Mozart Festival is held every summer in many cities in the United States. Classical music is performed in concert halls by choirs, instrumental groups, and soloists the world over. You may even hear Classical music used in television or radio commercials. Advertisers use the music to create a certain mood.

American Revolutionary War fought

1775–1783

Federal Government established in America

1789

1775

James Watt invents the steam engine

1789

French Revolution begins

1808

Roman excavations begin at Pompeii, Italy

1776

American Declaration of Independence signed

Check Your Understanding

Recall

1. What is the main difference between the Baroque and Classical styles?

2. What are the main characteristics of Classical music?

3. Name two composers who wrote during the Classical period.

4. What form was very important in instrumental compositions of the Classical period? Describe the form.

5. How did opera change during the Classical period?

Thinking It Through

1. How did the Greek and Roman cultures influence the Classical period?

2. Was the music of the Classical period enjoyed by all people, or by just the wealthy? Explain your answer.

3. If you wanted to hear examples of Classical music today, where could you find them?

4. Are there any similarities between characteristics of the Classical period and those of the society you live in today?

Listening to . . .
Classical Music

CHORAL SELECTION

Mozart—The Marriage of Figaro, Act I, (Scene 6) "Non so piu"

"Non so piu" from *The Marriage of Figaro* is an aria performed by Cherubino, a young page who is in love with love itself. *The Marriage of Figaro* (written in 1786), is a comic opera or "opera buffa" and revolves around the marriage of a valet, Figaro, and maid, Susanna. The plot has many comical confusions, jealousies and deceptions, The part of Cherubino is played by a soprano in a trouser role.

INSTRUMENTAL SELECTION

Mozart—*Eine kleine Nachtmusik,* First Movement

Translated, *Eine kleine Nachtmusik* means "A Little Night Music." Originally, it was written for a string quartet, but is now performed by major string orchestras. It was written to be played at a garden party or other social event where "small talk" needed to be filtered out.

Introducing...

"Dies Irae"

Wolfgang Amadeus Mozart

Setting the Stage

Composed in 1791 when Mozart was 35, "Dies Irae" is from the well-known *Requiem*. Mozart did not finish this multi-movement work before he died. He left sketches of some movements which were completed by one of his pupils, Sussmayr. Maintaining the refined quality found in music from the Classical period, Mozart uses the emotion of the rhythm and notes to create a fiery picture of the Day of Judgment. The accompaniment, originally for orchestra, is constantly moving—representing the flames of hell. The notes also help depict the exit ("Quantus tremor est futurus," the trembling figure in the bass part in measure 41 and in measures 49–51). The emotion of the scene is carried from the beginning to the end with a driving rhythm from both the chorus and the orchestra. This piece should be challenging and fulfilling for you to sing.

Meeting the Composer

Wolfgang Amadeus Mozart (1756–1791)

Born in Salzburg, Austria, Wolfgang Amadeus Mozart, whose full name is Johann Chrysostom Wolfgang Theophilus, began his musical career at an extremely early age. By the time he was four years old, Mozart had already mastered the keyboard and had written his first musical piece by age five. He became a master of the violin quickly thereafter. Mozart's father, Leopold Mozart, realized Amadeus' talent and began a tour through Europe, exhibiting his young son's extraordinary talents. By age 16, Mozart had already written about 25 symphonies. While writing the *Requiem*, Mozart was stricken with an illness that left him bedridden for the final three weeks of his life.

CLASSICAL LESSON

Dies Irae

From *Requiem*
COMPOSER: *Wolfgang Amadeus Mozart (1756–1791)*
ARRANGER: *Patrick Liebergen*

CHORAL MUSIC TERMS

allegro assai

choral blend

Classical period

unified vowels

Wolfgang Amadeus Mozart

VOICING

SAB

PERFORMANCE STYLE

Allegro assai

Accompanied by keyboard

FOCUS

- Use correct Latin pronunciation for the song text.
- Sing with a blended choral sound.

Warming Up

Vocal Warm-Up

Sing on solfège syllables, then on *low*. Listen carefully for all parts on the last chords. Hold each chord until it is tuned securely and there is balance between the parts. This exercise contains stepwise melody, a melody based on chord tones, and chords. Can you identify each of these parts? How can you tell when a chord has a good blend?

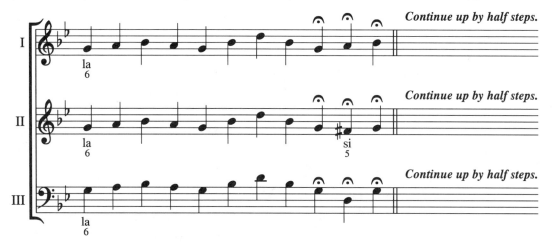

Sight-Singing

Sight-sing these parts using solfège syllables or numbers, then repeat on *low*. Try to keep the vowel unified among voices and the notes smoothly connected as you sing. Singing in tune and unified vowels are characteristics of a good blended sound.

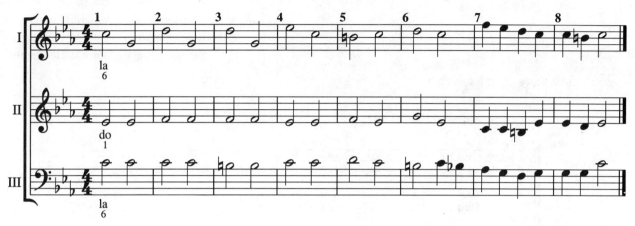

Singing: "Dies Irae"

Identify ingredients for making cookies. When you prepare cookies, these ingredients must be blended together. After they are mixed, most ingredients are no longer identifiable as they were in their original state. A choral blend has similar characteristics. All parts are equally mixed, and none is more identifiable than the others.

Now turn to the music for "Dies Irae" on page 166.

HOW DID YOU DO?

Think about your performance of the Vocal Warm-Up, Sight-Singing, and "Dies Irae."
1. Could you sing your part independently?
2. Describe the characteristics of a blended sound.
3. Did your sound blend with the rest of the group? How do you know?
4. How was your Latin pronunciation?
5. What characteristics of Classical music did you experience in this piece?
6. Did you find "Dies Irae" challenging? Why? Why not? Use specific musical terms and examples to explain.

Dies Irae

from "Requiem"

Music by Wolfgang Amadeus Mozart (1756–1791)
Edited and arranged by Patrick M. Liebergen
English setting by Patrick M. Liebergen

SAB Voices and Keyboard

† Text translation is paraphrased to accommodate the English language.

Emotional response is the significant feature in *Wounded Feelings* by English artist Alice Walker. Interest in exploring feelings and reactions, rather than formal structure, is typical of visual arts and music during the Romantic period.

1862. Alice Walker. *Wounded Feelings*. Oil on canvas. 101.6 x 76.2 cm (40 x 30"). The Forbes Magazine Collection, New York, New York.

Romantic Period

After completing this lesson, you will be able to:

- Compare qualities of music written in the Romantic and Classical styles.
- Identify two major composers from the Romantic period.
- Define nationalism, art songs, *and the* Romantic period.

Whenever there are rules, they are challenged by some people. The **Romantic period** (1820–1900) was *a time in which artists and composers attempted to make a break from classical music ideas.* The eighteenth century came to a close, leaving behind a restrained and controlled era, and the nineteenth century brought a newly acquired political and artistic freedom. There was a revolutionary spirit in society, with ideals of liberty and individualism, dramatic action, and indepentent thought. The musical restraints and order of the Classical period soon gave way to experimentation, as composers became impatient with the older rules and traditions.

The Romantic Period—a Time of Drama

Most composers of the Romantic period kept many of the classical forms alive. However, it is their treatment of these forms that made new statements about music. **Symphonies**—*large orchestral pieces for many instruments, usually of three or four parts or movements*—began to become popular. In some symphonies, a chorus was added (e.g., Beethoven's *Ninth Symphony*).

Many composers based their works on legends, dramas, or novels. In doing so, they explored through their music the heights and depths of human emotion. This innovation contrasted with previous vocal and instrumental works, many of which required musical simplicity. In general, vocal melodies became longer and more expressive, harmonies became more colorful, and instrumentation was expanded to enhance the overall possibilities of tone color in the music. Freedom and flexibility of rhythm and form brought new hues to the palette of sound composed by Romantic period composers.

Music of the Period

During the Romantic period, a new class of people—landowners, merchants, businesspeople who were not nobles—gained a powerful place in society. We refer to them as the middle class. With the help of the Industrial Revolution, which created many jobs, more and more people entered this class and took an active part in their culture and their nation. A growing pride in patriotism brought a spirit of nationalism to music. **Nationalism** in music

COMPOSERS

Ludwig van Beethoven (1770–1827)
Franz Schubert (1797–1828)
Hector Berlioz (1803–1869)
Felix Mendelssohn (1809–1847)
Frédéric Chopin (1810–1849)
Robert Schumann (1810–1856)
Franz Liszt (1811–1886)
Richard Wagner (1813–1883)
Giuseppe Verdi (1813–1901)
Clara Schumann (1819–1896)
Johannes Brahms (1833–1897)
Georges Bizet (1838–1875)
Modest Mussorgsky (1839–1881)
Peter Ilyich Tchaikovsky (1840–1893)
Giacomo Puccini (1858–1924)

ARTISTS

Élisabeth Vigée-Lebrun (1755–1842)
Rosa Bonheur (1822–1899)
Edouard Manet (1832–1883)
Edgar Degas (1834–1917)
Paul Cezanne (1839–1906)
Claude Monet (1840–1926)
Berthe Morisot (1841–1895)
Pierre Auguste Renoir (1841–1919)
Mary Cassatt (1845–1926)
Vincent van Gogh (1853–1890)
Georges Seurat (1859–1891)
Alice Walker (1944–)

AUTHORS

Noah Webster (1758–1843)
Mary Wollstonecraft Shelley (1797–1851)
Ralph Waldo Emerson (1803–1882)
Elizabeth Barrett Browning (1806–1861)
Henry Wadsworth Longfellow (1807–1882)
Edgar Allan Poe (1809–1849)
Harriet Beecher Stowe (1811–1896)
Theodore Dostoyevsky (1821–1881)
Leo Tolstoy (1828–1910)

CHORAL MUSIC TERMS

art songs
nationalism
Romantic period
symphonies

Louisiana Purchase
established

▼ **1803**

Abraham Lincoln

▼ **1809–1865**

Frederick Douglass

▼ **c. 1817–1895**

Mary Baker Eddy

▼ **1821–1910**

Monroe Doctrine created

▼ **1823**

▲ **1804**

Napoleon crowned Emperor

▲ **1812–1814**

U.S. declares war on Britain

▲ **1821**

Jean Champollion deciphers Egyptian
hieroglyphics using the Rosetta Stone

**The glass-and-iron Crystal Palace was erected for
the 1851 Great Exhibition in Hyde Park, London.
Its naves and transepts housed the Handel
Orchestra and Choir, concert halls, and exhibits
of paintings and sculptures.**

1851. Vincent Brooks. Crystal Palace. Lithograph. Victoria and Albert Museum,
London, Great Britain.

means that composers created works that evoked *pride in a country's historical and legendary past*. Richard Wagner wanted to preserve German music and legends in his operas. Giuseppe Verdi, great Italian composer of opera, felt he should guide the younger generation to adhere to the Italian historical and cultural tradition. This nationalism spawned interest in folk music of particular nations and regions. Robert Schumann used or imitated German folk songs. The American composer Stephen Foster composed songs on themes of life in the southern United States.

The art song became the most important vocal form during the Romantic period. **Art songs** were *expressive songs about life, love, and human relationships for solo voice and piano*. The most prolific composer of art songs, known in German as *lieder*, was Franz Schubert. Others were Robert Schumann and Johannes Brahms.

Modern Innovations

The idea of "selling" music to an audience through the musicians who composed it was developed during this time. In an effort to capture the general public's interest, a colorful and controversial personal life became an important factor in the visibility of many composers. Some of these composers were Franz Liszt, Hector Berlioz, and Richard Wagner.

Another figure to emerge in the performance setting was the music critic. His or her job was not only to explain the composer and the composer's music to the public, but also to set standards in musical taste.

Mary Mason Lyon founds Mt. Holyoke Female Seminary

▼ **1837**

Jane Addams and Ellen Starr
found Hull House

▼ **1889**

Motion picture camera patented by Thomas
Edison; sound recording developed

▼ **1898**

▲ **1835–1910**

Mark Twain

▲ **1844–1900**

Friedrich Nietzsche

▲ **1895**

Wireless telegraph developed by Marconi

The Romantic Period in Retrospect

The Romantic period was a time of exploration, imagination, and diversity. This period was diverse and complex, and it would be hard to describe with one definition all the new styles that emerged during it. The Romantic movement, however, was international in scope and influenced all the arts. The excitement of the Romantic period came from the rejection and challenge of old ways and a search for new, unique, and meaningful possibilities.

Check Your Understanding

Recall

1. Write one sentence which characterizes the mood of the Romantic period.

2. How did vocal melodies change during the Romantic period?

3. How did instrumental music change during the Romantic period?

4. Describe nationalism.

5. Define art song.

6. Name a Romantic composer of each: opera, art song.

Thinking It Through

1. Compare musical characteristics of the Classical and Romantic periods.

2. What was the role of the individual in music of the Romantic period?

3. Why was a music critic more likely to emerge during the Romantic period than before?

Listening to . . .

Romantic Music

CHORAL SELECTION

Bizet — *Carmen, Act I, "Habanera"*

Georges Bizet (1838–1875) composed the music for the opera *Carmen*, based on a novel written by Prosper Mérimée.

The story takes place in Seville, Spain, around 1820. Carmen is a gypsy girl who works in the tobacco factory. She is arrested for fighting, but Don José, a soldier, becomes infatuated with her and allows her to escape. Months later, they are reunited, but soon argue because Carmen insists he must leave the army to be with her. At first he refuses, but after a fight with an officer he decides he has no choice except to join her.

After he is with the gypsies for some time, however, Carmen tires of him and insists he return to town to care for his mother. Carmen then takes a new lover, Escamillo. Don José is devastated by her rejection and, jealous of Escamillo, ends up stabbing Carmen. If he can't have her, no one will!

INSTRUMENTAL SELECTION

Mussorgsky — *Pictures at an Exhibition, "The Hut on Fowl's Legs"/"The Great Gate of Kiev"*

Modest Mussorgsky (1839–1881) was a very good friend of Victor Hartmann, an architect, watercolorist, and designer. The year after Hartmann died, a grief-stricken Mussorgsky visited an exhibition of his works and then wrote ten musical sketches inspired by pictures he had seen in the Hartmann memorial show. "The Hut on Fowl's Legs" is a picture of a Russian folklore witch, Baba Yaga, and her enchanted house. "The Great Gate of Kiev" is a sketch of a gate to be built in honor of fallen Russian soldiers.

ROMANTIC CONNECTIONS

Introducing...

"In Stiller Nacht"

Johannes Brahms

Setting the Stage

"In Stiller Nacht" is an example of a folk song composed during the nationalist movement during the Romantic period. Within the confines of classical forms Brahms created new expressions in the warmth of the Romantic movement. Harmonies were expanded to add more color, making the phrases more expressive (measures 1–8). The addition of harmonic tension (measures 9–12) brings the emotion of the text to a new height of expression. The warmth of harmony and text will make this piece a pleasure to perform.

Meeting the Composer

Johannes Brahms (1833–1897)

Johannes Brahms is considered one of the leading composers of the Romantic period. His virtuosity in playing the piano stems from his early years when he helped support his family by performing in taverns and theaters. He also arranged popular waltzes for a local publisher. Brahms composed symphonies and overtures for orchestras as well as a wealth of choral pieces with piano and orchestral accompaniment. One of his finest works is A *German Requiem* which was written following the death of his mother. Brahms songs for voices(s) and piano are among the most delightful and accessible to all. Based on folk melodies or themselves folk songs, these compositions are full of emotion and delight.

In Stiller Nacht

COMPOSER: *Johannes Brahms* (1833–1897)
ARRANGER: *David L. Weck*

CHORAL MUSIC TERMS
articulation
crescendo
decrescendo

VOICING
SAT

PERFORMANCE STYLE
Somewhat slowly
Accompanied by piano

FOCUS
- Detached and connected articulation.
- Use correct German pronunciation for the song text.
- Sustained crescendo and decrescendo.

Warming Up

Vocal Warm-Up 1

Sing on *loo*. Notice the dynamic markings. Working with a partner, face one another, and stand with one foot in front of the other, clasping hands. As you begin to sing the crescendo, pull outward with even tension between you and your partner. Feel the "pull" of the phrase as you connect the notes together. What will the appropriate movement be during the decrescendo?

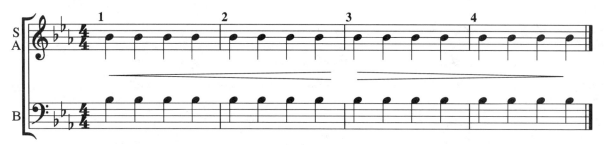

Vocal Warm-Up 2

Sing on solfège syllables, then on *hoh*. Notice the articulation markings. Sing the first four notes detached, and the second four on one connected sound. Whether you sing detached or connected pitches, maintain your breath support.

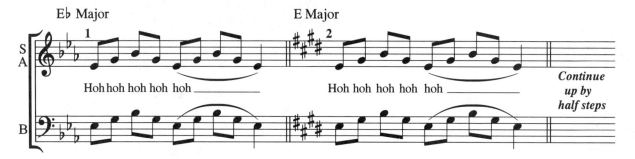

Sight-Singing

Everyone sight-sings the tenor part first, using solfège syllables and hand signs or numbers. Then sing all the parts. First sing with separated notes, then connect the notes carefully together.

Singing: "In Stiller Nacht"

If you were living with a family who did not speak your language, how would you communicate something that made you very sad?

If you could speak a little of their language, what would you do to make sure you were clearly understood?

Now turn to the music for "In Stiller Nacht" on page 184.

HOW DID YOU DO? ？ ？	Think about your performance on the Vocal Warm-Ups, Sight-Singing, and "In Stiller Nacht." **1.** Could you sing your part independently? **2.** Describe how you used dynamics to shape the phrase. **3.** Describe how you used articulation to interpret the piece.	**4.** How was your German pronunciation? **5.** What characteristics of Romantic music did you experience in this piece? **6.** Do you think the music fits the text of "In Stiller Nacht"? Why? Why not? Use specific musical terms and language to support your opinion.

In Stiller Nacht

Johannes Brahms
Arranged by David L. Weck
English words by H.T. Duffield, alt.

SAT Voices and Accompaniment

Three Musicians, a Cubist work by Pablo Picasso (1881–1973), demonstrates visual art based on geometric elements. In art and music, contemporary artists employ a variety of new techniques in the creation of their works.

1921. Pablo Picasso. *Three Musicians*. (Detail.) Oil on canvas. 200.7 x 222.9 cm (6'7" x 7'3¾"). Museum of Modern Art, New York, New York. Mrs. Simon Guggenheim Fund.

Contemporary Period

After completing this lesson, you will be able to:

- Compare qualities of music written in the Romantic and Contemporary styles.
- Identify several characteristics and styles of twentieth-century music.
- Define dissonance, twelve-tone music, *and* aleatoric, *or* chance music.
- Define fusion.

You live in the **Contemporary period,** *the time from* 1900 *to right now*, so you know something about contemporary music. More likely, however, there are some kinds of contemporary music that are still awaiting your discovery. One of the most important characteristics of the twentieth century has been rapid change. In this century, humans have lived through two world wars, the Chinese and Russian revolutions, the Great Depression, the Cold War, the rise and fall of Communism in many countries of the world, and many other events. Society is moving fast, and changes are constant.

A Time of Variety

Technology has had a large influence in the twentieth century, and it affects the preferences and demands of people. First, phonographs made music easily accessible to anyone who wanted to hear it. The invention of the radio brought live performances right into people's homes. Then, television captivated the world. Now tape recorder/players, CDs, and computers with interactive programs are popular, bringing us higher quality sounds and images and more possibilities. In many locations, synthesizers are taking the place of acoustic instruments, making it less expensive and easier for everyone to be involved in music-making and listening.

Looking Back

In the Romantic period, composers searched for new means of musical expression through the use of changed musical elements and larger orchestras. Many times, they were painting a story or mood in sound. As we have seen in the past, the artistic cycle tends to go from emotional to rational and back. During the twentieth century, composers and artists looked toward the abstract as a reaction to the overly emotional Romantic arts. They felt music was its own justification—it did not exist to paint some picture or evoke some emotion. Consequently, great changes occurred.

COMPOSERS

Richard Strauss (1864–1949)
Ralph Vaughan Williams (1872–1958)
Charles Ives (1874–1954)
Béla Bartók (1881–1945)
Igor Stravinsky (1882–1971)
Sergei Prokofiev (1891–1953)
George Gershwin (1898–1937)
Aaron Copland (1900–1990)
Benjamin Britten (1913–1976)
Leonard Bernstein (1918–1990)
David N. Davenport
Eugene Butler
Bob Dylan (1941–)

ARTISTS

Henri Rousseau (1844–1910)
Wassily Kandinsky (1866–1944)
Henri Matisse (1869–1954)
Pablo Picasso (1881–1973)
Georgia O'Keeffe (1887–1986)
Jackson Pollock (1912–1956)
Andrew Wyeth (1917–)
Andy Warhol (1930–1987)

AUTHORS

George Bernard Shaw (1856–1950)
Sir Arthur Conan Doyle (1859–1930)
Edith Wharton (1862–1937)
Gertrude Stein (1874–1946)
Robert Frost (1874–1963)
James Joyce (1882–1941)
Virginia Woolf (1882–1941)
T. S. Eliot (1888–1965)
William Faulkner (1897–1962)
Ernest Hemingway (1899–1961)
John Steinbeck (1902–1968)
Maya Angelou (1928–)

CHORAL MUSIC TERMS

abstract
aleatoric music
chance music
Contemporary period
dissonance
fusion
twelve-tone music

Wright Brothers' flight

1903

Model-T Ford introduced

1908

1905

First motion picture
theater opens

1914–1918

World War I

▲ **Just as contemporary music explores new avenues of expression, the Chapel of Notre Dame du Haut is a unique style of architecture. The massive walls and the rounded roof reflect abstract sculpture of contemporary artists. At the same time, the design is suggestive of the strength and solidity of a medieval fortress.**

1955. Le Corbusier. Frontal view of Chapelle de Notre Dame du Haut. Chapelle de Notre Dame du Haut, Ronchamp, France.

During the Romantic period, there was a change from church- and patron-sponsored composition to commissions and the sale of compositions. As the emerging middle class became the main consumer of music, the aristocracy played a less important role. Musicians' income was now provided by the sale of concert tickets and published music. In the twentieth century, serious music is supported by large and small performing groups in most cities and large towns. There is also support from nonprofit organizations, colleges, and universities.

As the twentieth century draws to a close, we can look back and see the changes from Impressionism (music that creates a musical picture with a

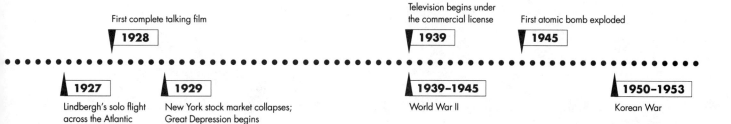

First complete talking film

1928

Television begins under
the commercial license

1939

First atomic bomb exploded

1945

1927

Lindbergh's solo flight
across the Atlantic

1929

New York stock market collapses;
Great Depression begins

1939–1945

World War II

1950–1953

Korean War

dreamy quality through chromaticism) to Expressionism (bold and dynamic expression of mood with great dissonance). Composers still use some forms from the Romantic period, such as opera, the symphony, and song form. Yet, they also continue to experiment with new ways to express themselves through music.

Music of the Period

Much of the music written before World War I was a continuation of Romanticism. After that war, composers were striving for a more objective style, a style stressing music for its own sake. There was a swing toward the **abstract,** *focusing on lines, rows, angles, clusters, textures, and form.*

Prior to the twentieth century, chords were built in intervals of a third. In the twentieth century, composers moved away from a tonal center and scalewise organization of pitch, and built *chords using seconds, fourths, fifths, and sevenths.* This resulted in a **dissonance** that sounded very harsh to those accustomed to tonal music.

Twelve-tone music was a new organization for composition. In twelve-tone music, *the twelve tones of the chromatic scale are arranged in a tone row, then the piece is composed by arranging and rearranging the "row" in different ways—backward, forward, in clusters of three or four pitches, and so on.* The mathematical possibilities are almost endless, especially when layered, instrument over instrument. Many people feel that music composed this way is more of an exercise for the composer than a source of pleasure for the listener.

Another interesting experimental type of music is **aleatoric,** or **chance music.** In aleatoric music, *the piece has a beginning and an end, and the rest is left to chance.* There is usually a score of some kind, but great freedom is allowed each performer (for example, how long to hold each pitch, which pitch to begin on, how fast to go, and when to stop).

Other compositional elements of the twentieth century include more angular contour of the melody and different concepts of harmony, which may emphasize dissonance, complex rhythms, and specific performance markings.

World Music and Fusion

During the twentieth century, folk music from around the world traveled to greater distances as people became more mobile. Immigrants and travelers shared songs from diverse cultures, and the musical styles have influenced one another. Popular music styles emerged and continue to be created, based on characteristics of different folk groups and the intermingling of ideas. Serious

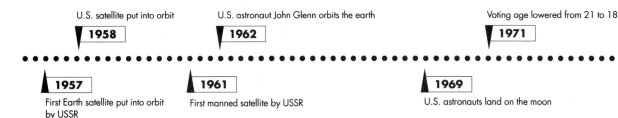

U.S. satellite put into orbit

1958

U.S. astronaut John Glenn orbits the earth

1962

Voting age lowered from 21 to 18

1971

1957

First Earth satellite put into orbit by USSR

1961

First manned satellite by USSR

1969

U.S. astronauts land on the moon

music composers also used the characteristics, melodies, and texts of folk music for their compositions. *Musical styles began to blend* in a phenomenon called **fusion.** For example, African-American, Cajun, and French Canadian musics have blended to create the fusion style called zydeco. This kind of fusion is continuing today around the world.

There is also fusion of popular and art music styles. Many folk songs are being arranged and played by symphony orchestras. For example, vocalist Bobby McFerrin collaborated with classical cellist Yo-Yo Ma in recordings and performances with symphony orchestras. Popular singers such as Linda Ronstadt and Sting perform with professional choirs and orchestras. Instruments from many cultures find their way into classical performing groups, and music from all periods is being rearranged for electronic media.

Contemporary Pop Styles

Listed below are some American styles that have emerged during the twentieth century. Some of them are still thriving, and new ones are being created every day.

- *Ragtime*—an early style of jazz, very rhythmic and syncopated.
- *Musical Stage Music*—centered around Broadway and Hollywood musicals.
- *Blues*—simple, harmonious melodies with two phrases the same, then one different.
- *Spiritual*—songs originating in the slave culture, usually religious in theme.
- *Jazz*—strong but rhythmic understructure supporting solo and ensemble improvisation.
- *Rock*—strong, steady beat.
- *Country*—based on the folk style of the southern rural United States or on the music of the cowboy.
- *Folk*—folk songs and composed songs that tell a story or sometimes have a social message.
- *Reggae*—a fusion of rock and Jamaican rhythms, instruments, and language.
- *Calypso*—an island style with strong chords and syncopation.
- *Tejano*—a fusion of Mexican and country music.
- *Zydeco*—a fusion of African-American, Cajun, and French Canadian rhythms, instruments, and lyrics.

Music's Future and You

It is important that the consumer—that's you—has a sense of quality, in both popular and classical music. That way, quality music will survive into the future.

Little League accepts girls

1975

Fall of the Berlin Wall

1989

1972

Robert Moog patents the
Moog synthesizer

1975

U.S. withdraws from Vietnam

1976

U.S. celebrates its 200th birthday

Check Your Understanding

Recall

1. What technological inventions made music more accessible during the twentieth century?

2. Why did music change during the Contemporary period?

3. Are any forms from past periods still being composed? How are they different?

4. Describe dissonance.

5. Describe twelve-tone and aleatoric music.

6. Why is folk music still sung in the twentieth century? Name a folk song you have heard that is a twentieth-century piece.

7. Describe the result of fusion.

Thinking It Through

1. Some people say that records, tapes, and CDs are bad for society, because people never get together to sing or go out to concerts anymore. Do you think this is true? Why or why not? How do they affect the way we appreciate music?

2. If you wanted to see and hear examples of Contemporary art and popular music today, where could you find them?

Listening to . . .
Contemporary Music

CHORAL SELECTION

Bob Dylan — "Mister Tambourine Man"

Bob Dylan was a prolific protest songwriter of the 1960s and 1970s. He wrote and performed music in a folk style. The Byrds, who performed "Mister Tambourine Man" on the recording you will hear, was a rock group from California. Dylan's folk style, combined with the Byrds' rock style, produced a new strand of music called "Folk Rock." "Mister Tambourine Man" was the Byrds' biggest hit and released a new wave of folk rock music that influenced songwriters in the following decades.

INSTRUMENTAL SELECTION

Britten — *The Young Person's Guide to the Orchestra*

(Variations and Fugue on a Theme of Purcell)

Benjamin Britten (1913–1976) was an English composer whose abilities and precociousness led him to be compared to Mozart's genius. He was commissioned by the English Ministry of Education to write a unique work for children to teach them the instruments of the orchestra. He took a theme from Henry Purcell's incidental music to *Abdelazar* and created *The Young Person's Guide to the Orchestra* that included a theme, variations and fugue.

CONTEMPORARY CONNECTIONS

Introducing . . .
"River, Sing Your Song"

David N. Davenport

Setting the Stage

"River, Sing Your Song" by David N. Davenport is an example of twentieth century choral music that is written in the style of folk music. What might have been a solo or pop song has been harmonized and turned into wonderful choral literature. The public schools, colleges, and universities have had a tremendous influence and demand for this type of music.

Meeting the Composer

David N. Davenport and Eugene Butler

A graduate of Indiana University, Davenport has directed junior high, high school, and church choirs for many years. The thrill of hearing his first composition sung by a 300-person choir encouraged Davenport to continue writing songs. Many of his choral music songs are "mood pieces" that deal with subject matter taken from the natural elements. For example, "Sea Scenes," published some years ago, paints a musical picture of the ocean and how it moves. Another song, "Willow, Willow," deals with willow trees, whose branches are flowing gracefully in the wind. He wrote the text for "River, Sing Your Song," and then asked Eugene Butler to put music to his words.

River, Sing Your Song

COMPOSER: *Eugene Butler*
TEXT: *David N. Davenport*

CHORAL MUSIC TERMS
dynamics
forte
mezzo forte (*mf*)

VOICING
Three-part mixed

PERFORMANCE STYLE
Flowing
Accompanied by piano

FOCUS
- Demonstrate correct dynamics.
- Determine and perform correct phrasing.

Warming Up

Vocal Warm-Up

Sing on solfège syllables, then on the neutral syllables under the notes. Notice the slurs. Usually a phrase is marked by a long arc. In this exercise there are short arcs that tell you to slur two pitches. But where would you mark the phrase? Sing through each phrase with strong breath support.

Sight-Singing

Sight-sing the parts below separately, then in any combination. How many phrases are in this exercise? Sing each phrase with a crescendo to the "peak," and then decrescendo to the end. What do the I, IV, V markings denote?

Singing: "River, Sing Your Song"

Can you improvise a melody that "describes" a river?

Listen to several classmates improvise a melody that "describes" a river. Choose one melody to sing all together.

With a partner, make up a simple movement that matches the melody.

Now turn to the music for "River, Sing Your Song" on page 196.

HOW DID YOU DO?

? ?

Think about your performance on the Vocal Warm-Up, Sight-Singing, and "River, Sing Your Song."
1. Could you describe your part independently?
2. Describe how you decided where each phrase begins and ends.
3. Describe how you used dynamics to enhance the phrases.

4. What characteristics of Contemporary music did you experience in this piece?
5. Do you think the music fits the text of "River, Sing Your Song"? Why? Why not? Use specific musical terms and language to support your opinion.

River, Sing Your Song

Eugene Butler
David N. Davenport

Three-part Mixed Voices, Accompanied

Wind - ing to the deep blue sea, O, riv - er, sing your

Wind - ing to the deep blue_ sea, O, riv - er, sing your

Wind - ing to the deep blue sea, O, riv - er, sing your

song for me.

song for me.

song for me.

mf

Rip-pling riv - er on your way

Rip-pling riv - er on your way

Rip-pling riv - er on your way

Through the dark - ness and the day, Sing your gen - tle

Through the dark - ness and the day, __ Sing your gen - tle

Through the dark - ness and the __ day, Sing your gen - tle

mel - o -dy, O, riv - er, sing your song for me.

mel - o -dy, O, riv - er, sing your song for me.

mel - o - dy, O, riv - er, sing your song for me.

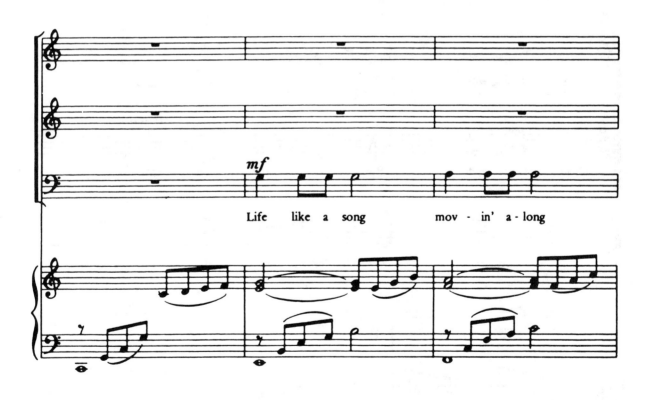

mf

Life like a song mov - in' a - long

Tossed by the sea,

Tossed by the sea,

flows like the on - go - ing tide.

blown in the wind, Riv - er, stay by my side.

blown in the wind, Riv - er, stay by my side.

Riv - er, stay by my side.

Additional Performance Selections

VOICING
SATB

PERFORMANCE STYLE
Purposeful
Accompanied by piano

I Hear Liberty Singing

Warming Up

Vocal Warm-Up
Sing the pattern using solfège syllables or numbers. Then switch to singing on *loo*. Hold the last chord and move one half-step up to a new key. Continue the exercise, moving one half-step up on each repeat.

Continue up by half steps.

Now turn to page 207.

VOICING
SAB

PERFORMANCE STYLE
Pensive
Accompanied by piano

It's Time to Fly Away

Warming Up

Vocal Warm-Up
Sing the following patterns using solfège or numbers.

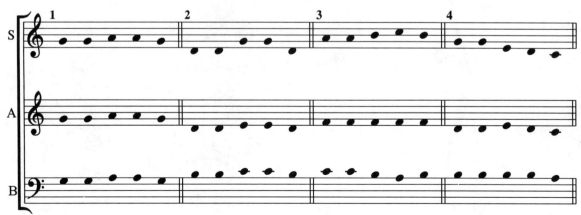

Now turn to page 216.

Shenandoah

Warming Up

Vocal Warm-Up

Practice these intervals up and down by half steps. Sing using solfège or numbers. Do each key section all on one breath.

Now turn to page **223.**

Three Yoruba Native Songs of Nigeria

Warming Up

Vocal Warm-Up

Sing using solfège or numbers. Continue to move up stepwise.

Now turn to page **231.**

VOICING

SAB

PERFORMANCE STYLE

Moderato
Accompanied by piano

The Tree of Peace

Warming Up

Vocal Warm-Up

Sing the parts below in G minor using solfège. Notice where the parts are in unison, and where there are two and three parts. The chord tones are sometimes close together, so listen carefully.

Now turn to page **234.**

206 *Choral Connections   Level 1 Mixed Voices*

I Hear Liberty Singing

Words and Music by
GREG GILPIN

SATB, Accompanied

ta-tion.   One voice,   sing-ing all a - lone.   Through the

years,   ma-ny marched a-gainst___ her. And they mocked the mes-sage that she

sang.   And they fought   so they could keep her si - lent. And

turned so they could not see her flame. But I hear li-ber-ty

sing-ing. Her song of free-dom is ring-ing a-round the

world, strong-er than be-fore. From shore to shore, I hear li-ber-ty

Oo

I hear li-ber-ty

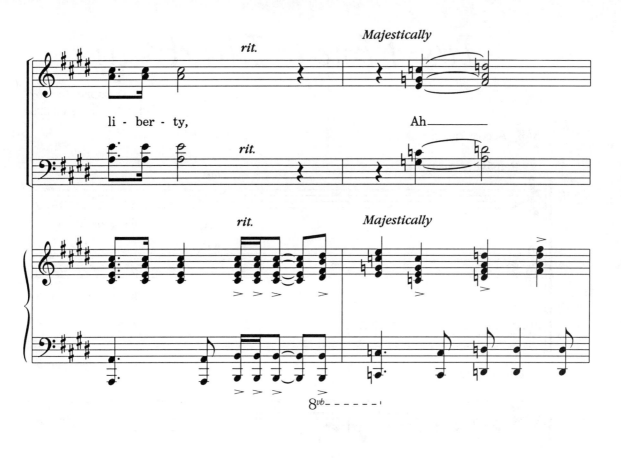

li - ber - ty,

Ah_____

li - ber - ty

sings!_____

It's Time to Fly Away

Words and Music by
JOYCE ELAINE EILERS

SAB, Accompanied

V 7909 - 2

all who would lis-ten, he sends his — song, and then he flies a -

all who would lis-ten, he sends his — song, and then he flies a -

all who would lis-ten, he sends his song, and then he flies a -

F   F/D   G/E   Am   F/D   Gsus   G

12 *mf* **Slight quickening** (♩ = 96)

way. _____ Song - bird, the

mf

way. _____ Song - bird, the

mf

way. _____ Song - bird, the

C   C   12 **Slight quickening** (♩ = 96)
F   G

slight accel. _   *mf*

time   to fly   a - way. _____

time   to fly   a - way. _____

time   to fly   a - way. _____

37   F/D   F/G   A♭   B♭   C

rit. - - - - - - - - - - - - - -

rit. - - - - - - - - - - - - - -

rit. - - - - - - - - - - - - - -

(A - way.) _____

rit. - - - - - - - - - - - - - -

V 7909

Optional - Solo or small group, Tenor or Alto.

222   *Choral Connections   Level 1 Mixed Voices*

Shenandoah

Traditional
American Folk Song
Arranged by Brad Printz

Three-part Mixed Chorus and Piano

Reproduced by permission. Permit #275772.

your peace - ful val - ley, _____ a -

way _____ you roll - in' riv - er.

_mf_
A - way, you roll - in' riv - er.

_mf_

I long to see _____ your peace - ful

I long to see your peace - ful

I long to see your _____

Three Yoruba Native Songs of Nigeria

Arranged by
Henry H. Leck and Prince Julius Adeniyi

Unison Voiced and Percussion

1. E ORU O
"Greeting"

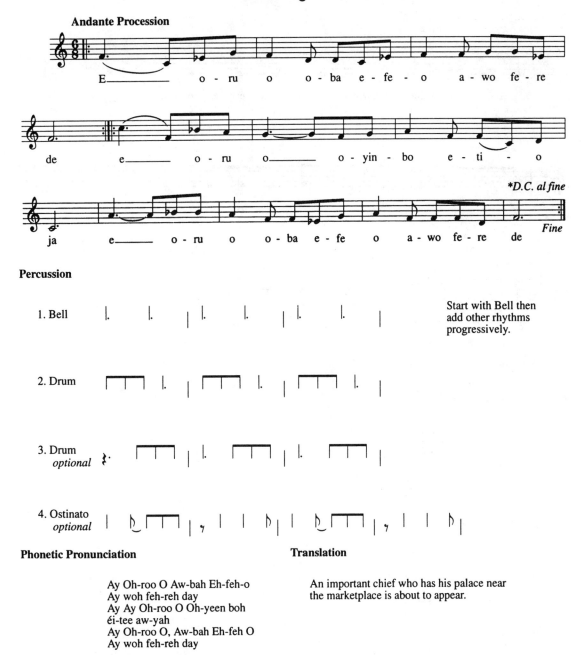

Phonetic Pronunciation

Ay Oh-roo O Aw-bah Eh-feh-o
Ay woh feh-reh day
Ay Ay Oh-roo O Oh-yeen boh
éi-tee aw-yah
Ay Oh-roo O, Aw-bah Eh-feh O
Ay woh feh-reh day

Translation

An important chief who has his palace near
the marketplace is about to appear.

* The number of times the song is repeated is left to the discretion of the director.

2. ODUN DE
"New Year is Here"

O - dun de o - dun de_____ o - dun de an - y - o_____

_____ o - dun de an - y - o e du mar e jo wo wa gbo pe wa o

ir e ir e_____ e e e e e o - dun de e

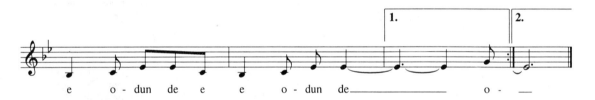

e o - dun de e e o - dun de_____ o - _____

Same Percussion Rhythm Patterns As "E Oru O"

Phonetic Pronunciation

> Aw-doon day aw-doon day
> Aw-doon day ahn-your
> Ay doo-mah ray ja-war wah (g) baw peh
> Wah o
> Eer-ay eer-ay ay ay ay ay ay ay
> Aw-doon day ay aw-doon day ay
> Aw-doon day

Translation

> New Year is here, New Year is here
> We are happy. Almighty God.
> Please accept our thanks. Blessing, blessing
> New Year is here, New Year is here

3. KABO KABO
"Song of Praise in honor of a Prince or King"

Ka bo___ ka - bo ka - bo - ka - bo o mo-a ba - le

so - ro o mo-a ba - le so - ro ki - le la nu ka - bo. Ka - bo. A

ko bi a la ke lon jo ba la ke a ko bi ku___ ku lon

jo bi ni je bu-o de ka - bo___ ka -

bo ka - bo___ ka - bo o mo-a ba - le

so - ro o mo-a ba - le so - ro ki - le la nu ka - bo

Percussion

1. Djembe

2. Claves

3. Conga
R L R R L R

4. Bells

Translation	Phonetic Pronunciation
Welcome! Welcome! The son (prince) who speaks to the ground and makes the ground open	Kah-boh-o kah-boh o *(sing 2 times)* aw-maw ah-bah leh saw raw *(sing 2 times)* Kee-leh lah noo kah-boh
Verse: The first son of Alake (king) becomes the king of Ake (a city in Nigeria)	Ah-kaw bee ah lah kay lown jaw bah lah kay, Ah-kaw bee koo koo lown jaw bah nee-jeh-boo oh-day
Now the first son of Ku Ku (another king) becomes the king of Ijebuode (a city in Nigeria)	
Refrain: Kabo...	

The Tree of Peace

Adapted by Fred Bock
(A.S.C.A.P.)
John Greenleaf Whittier

SAB, Accompanied

Each smile a hymn, each kind - ly deed a

prayer. _____

(Tacet)

Strongly

f Then shall all the shack-les fall off _ and the storm - y clang-or of

Strongly

*Girls 2nd time only - Boys both times

Glossary

Choral Music Terms

A

a cappella (ah-kah-PEH-lah) [It.] Unaccompanied vocal music.

accelerando (*accel.*) (ah-chel-leh-RAHN-doh) [It.] Gradually increasing the tempo.

accent Indicates the note is to be sung with extra force or stress. (>)

accidentals Signs used to indicate the raising or lowering of a pitch. A sharp (♯) alters a pitch by raising it one-half step; a flat (♭) alters a pitch by lowering it one-half step; a natural (♮) cancels a sharp or a flat.

accompaniment Musical material that supports another; for example, a piano or orchestra accompanying a choir or soloist.

adagio (ah-DAH-jee-oh) [It.] Slow tempo, but not as slow as largo.

al fine (ahl FEE-neh) [It.] To the end.

alla breve Indicates cut time; duple meter in which there are two beats per measure, the half note getting one beat.

allargando (*allarg.*) (ahl-ahr-GAHN-doh) [It.] To broaden, become slower.

aleatoric or chance music Music in which chance is deliberately used as a compositional component.

allegro (ah-LEH-groh) [It.] Brisk tempo; faster than moderato, slower than *vivace*.

allegro assai (ah-LEH-groh ah-SAH-ee) [It.] Very fast; in seventeenth-century music, the term can also mean "sufficiently fast."

altered pitch A note that does not belong to the scale of the work being performed.

alto The lower female voice; sometimes called contralto or mezzo-soprano.

anacrusis (a-nuh-KROO-suhs) [Gk.] *See* upbeat.

andante (ahn-DAHN-teh) [It.] Moderately slow; a walking tempo.

andante con moto (ahn-DAHN-teh kohn MOH-toh) [It.] A slightly faster tempo, "with motion."

animato Quick, lively; "animated."

aria (AHR-ee-uh) [It.] A song for a solo singer and orchestra, usually in an opera, oratorio, or cantata.

arpeggio (ahr-PEH-jee-oh) [It.] A chord in which the pitches are sounded successively, usually from lowest to highest; in broken style.

art song Expressive songs about life, love, and human relationships for solo voice and piano.

articulation Clarity in performance of notes and diction.

a tempo (ah TEM-poh) [It.] Return to the established tempo after a change.

B

balance and symmetry Even and equal.

baritone The male voice between tenor and bass.

bar line (measure bar) A vertical line drawn through the staff to show the end of a measure. Double bar lines show the end of a section or a piece of music.

Bar Line   Double Bar Line

Baroque period (buh-ROHK) [Fr.] Historic period between c. 1600 and c. 1750 that reflected highly embellished styles in art, architecture, fashion, manners, and music. The period of elaboration.

bass The lowest male voice, below tenor and baritone.

bass clef Symbol at the beginning of the staff for lower voices and instruments, or the piano left hand; usually referring to pitches lower than middle C. The two dots lie on either side of the fourth-line F, thus the term, F clef.

beat A steady pulse.

bel canto (bell KAHN-toh) [It.] Italian vocal technique of the eighteenth century with emphasis on beauty of sound and brilliance of performance.

binary form Defines a form having two sections (A and B), each of which may be repeated.

breath mark A mark placed within a phrase or melody showing where the singer or musician should breathe. (')

C

cadence Punctuation or termination of a musical phrase; a breathing break.

caesura (si-ZHUR-uh) [Lt.] A break or pause between two musical phrases. (//)

call and response A song style that follows a simple question-and-answer pattern in which a soloist leads and a group responds.

calypso style Folk-style music from the Caribbean Islands with bright, syncopated rhythm.

cambiata The young male voice that is still developing.

canon   A compositional form in which the subject is begun in one group and then is continually and exactly repeated by other groups. Unlike the round, the canon closes with all voices ending together on a common chord.

cantata   (kan-TAH-tuh) [It.] A collection of vocal compositions with instrumental accompaniment consisting of several movements based on related secular or sacred text segments.

cantabile   In a lyrical, singing style.

chantey   (SHAN-tee) [Fr.] A song sung by sailors in rhythm with their work.

chant, plainsong   Music from the liturgy of the early church, characterized by free rhythms, monophonic texture, and sung *a cappella*.

chorale   (kuh-RAL) [Gr.] Congregational song or hymn of the German Protestant (Evangelical) Church.

chord   Three or more pitches sounded simultaneously.

chord, block   Three or more pitches sounded simultaneously.

chord, broken   Three or more pitches sounded in succession; *see also* arpeggio.

chromatic   (kroh-MAT-ik) [Gr.] Moving up or down by half steps. Also the name of a scale composed entirely of half steps.

Classical period   The period in Western history beginning around 1750 and lasting until around 1820 that reflected a time when society began looking to the ancient Greeks and Romans for examples of order and ways of looking at life.

clef   The symbol at the beginning of the staff that identifies a set of pitches; *see also* bass clef and treble clef.

coda   Ending section; a concluding portion of a composition. (⊕)

common time   Another name for 4/4 meter; *see also* cut time. (c)

composer   The creator of musical works.

compound meter   Meter whose beat can be subdivided into threes and/or sixes.

con   (kohn) [It.] With.

concerto   Composition for solo instrument and an orchestra, usually with three movements.

consonance   A musical interval or chord that sounds pleasing; opposite of dissonance.

Contemporary period   The time from 1900 to right now.

continuo   A Baroque tradition in which the bass line is played "continuously," by a cello, double bass, and/or bassoon while a keyboard instrument (harpsichord, organ) plays the bass line and indicated harmonies.

contrapuntal   *See* counterpoint.

counterpoint   The combination of simultaneous parts; *see* polyphony.

crescendo   (*cresc.*) (kreh-SHEN-doh) [It.] To gradually become louder.

cued notes   Smaller notes indicating either optional harmony or notes from another voice part.

cut time   2/2 time with the half note getting the beat. (¢)

D

da capo   (*D.C.*) (dah KAH-poh) [It.] Go back to the beginning and repeat; *see also* dal segno and al fine.

dal segno   (*D.S.*) (dahl SAYN-yoh) [It.] Go back to the sign and repeat. (※)

D. C. al fine   (dah KAH-poh ahl FEE-neh) [It.] Repeat back to the beginning and end at the "fine."

decrescendo   (*decresc.*) (deh-kreh-SHEN-doh) [It.] To gradually become softer.

delicato   Delicate; to play or sing delicately.

descant   A high, ornamental voice part often lying above the melody.

diction   Clear and correct enunciation.

diminuendo   (*dim.*) (duh-min-yoo-WEN-doh) [It.] Gradually getting softer; *see also* decrescendo.

diphthong   A combination of two vowel sounds consisting of a primary vowel sound and a secondary vowel sound. The secondary vowel sound is (usually) at the very end of the diphthong; for example, in the word *toy*, the diphthong starts with the sound of "o," then moves on to "y," in this case pronounced "ee."

dissonance   Discord in music, suggesting a state of tension or "seeking"; chords using seconds, fourths, fifths, and sevenths; the opposite of consonance.

divisi   (*div.*) (dih-VEE-see) [It.] Divide; the parts divide.

dolce   (DOHL-chay) [It.] Sweet; *dolcissimo*, very sweet; *dolcemente*, sweetly.

Dorian mode   A scale with the pattern of whole-step, half, whole, whole, whole, half, and whole. For example, D to D on the keyboard.

dotted rhythm   A note written with a dot increases its value again by half.

double bar   Two vertical lines placed on the staff indicating the end of a section or a composition; used with two dots to enclose repeated sections.

doubling   The performance of the same note by two parts, either at the same pitch or an octave apart.

downbeat   The accented first beat in a measure.

D. S. al coda   (dahl SAYN-yoh ahl KOH-dah) [It.] Repeat from the symbol (𝄋) and skip to the coda when you see the sign. (⊕)

D. S. al fine   (dahl SAYN-yoh ahl FEE-neh) [It.] Repeat from the symbol (𝄋) and sing to fine or the end.

duple   Any time signature or group of beats that is a multiple of two.

duet   Composition for two performers.

dynamics   The volume of sound, the loudness or softness of a musical passage; intensity, power.

E

enharmonic   Identical tones that are named and written differently; for example, C sharp and D flat.

ensemble   A group of musicians or singers who perform together.

enunciation   Speaking and singing words with distinct vowels and consonants.

espressivo   (*espress.*) (es-preh-SEE-vo) [It.] For expression; *con espressione*, with feeling.

ethnomusicology   The musical study of specific world cultures.

expressive singing   To sing with feeling.

exuberance   Joyously unrestrained and enthusiastic.

F

fermata   (fur-MAH-tah) [It.] A hold; to hold the note longer. (⌢)

fine   (FEE-neh) Ending; to finish.

flat   Symbol (accidental) that lowers a pitch by one half step. (♭)

folk music   Uncomplicated music that speaks directly of everyday matters; the first popular music; usually passed down through the oral tradition.

form   The structure of a musical composition.

forte   (*f*) (FOR-teh) [It.] Loud.

fortissimo   (*ff*) (for-TEE-suh-moh) [It.] Very loud.

freely   A direction that permits liberties with tempo, dynamics, and style.

fugue   (FYOOG) [It.] A polyphonic composition consisting of a series of successive melody imitations; *see also* imitative style.

fusion   A combination or blending of different genres of music.

G

gapped scale   A scale resulting from leaving out certain tones (the pentatonic scale is an example).

grand staff   Two staves usually linked together by a long bar line and a bracket.

H

half step   The smallest distance (interval) between two notes on a keyboard; the chromatic scale is composed entirely of half steps, shown as (v).

half time   *See* cut time.

harmonic interval   Intervals that are sung or played simultaneously; *see also* melodic interval.

harmony   Vertical blocks of different tones sounded simultaneously.

hemiola   (hee-mee-OH-lah) [Gk.] A metric flow of two against a metric flow of three.

$$\frac{6}{4} \; \text{♩. ♩. | ♩ ♩ ♩ |} \quad \text{or} \quad \frac{3}{4} \; \text{♩. | ♩. | ♩ ♩♩ ♩}$$

homophonic   (hah-muh-FAH-nik) [Gk.] A texture where all parts sing similar rhythm in unison or harmony.

homophony   (hah-MAH-fuh-nee) [Gk.] Music that consists of two or more voice parts with similar or identical rhythms. From the Greek words meaning "same sounds," homophony could be described as "hymn-style."

hushed   A style marking indicating a soft, whispered tone.

I

imitation, imitative style   Restating identical or nearly identical musical material in two or more parts.

improvised   Invented on the spur of the moment.

improvisation   Spontaneous musical invention, commonly associated with jazz.

interval   The distance from one note to another; intervals are measured by the total steps and half steps between the two notes.

intonation   The degree to which pitch is accurately produced in tune.

introduction   An opening section at the beginning of a movement or work, preparatory to the main body of the form.

key The way tonality is organized around a tonal center; *see also* key signature.

key change Changing an initial key signature in the body of a composition.

key signature Designation of sharps or flats at the beginning of a composition to indicate its basic scale and tonality.

legato (leh-GAH-toh) [It.] Smooth, connected style.

ledger lines Short lines that appear above, between treble and bass clefs, or below the bass clef, used to expand the notation.

[musical notation]

leggiero (leh-JEH-roh) [It.] Articulate lightly; sometimes nonlegato.

linear flow, line Singing/playing notes in a flowing (smooth) manner, as if in a horizontal line.

lullaby A cradle song; in Western music, usually sung with a gentle and regular rhythm.

M

madrigal A secular vocal form in several parts, popular in the Renaissance.

maestoso (mah-eh-STOH-soh) [It.] Perform majestically.

major (key, scale, mode) Scale built on the formula of two whole steps, one half step, three whole steps, one half step.

Letter Names:	G	A	B	C	D	E	F♯	G
Movable Do:	do	re	mi	fa	so	la	ti	do
Numbers:	1	2	3	4	5	6	7	1

Major 2nd The name for an interval of one whole step or two half steps. For example, from C to D.

Major 6th The name for an interval of four whole steps and one-half step. For example, from C to A.

Major 3rd The name for an interval of two whole steps or four half steps. For example, from C to E.

major triad Three tones that form a major third *do* to *mi* and a minor third *mi* to *so* as in C E G.

marcato (mahr-KAH-toh) [It.] Long but separated pitches; translated as marked.

mass The main religious service of the Roman Catholic Church. There are two divisions of mass: the Proper of the Mass in which the text changes for each day, and the Ordinary of the Mass in which the text remains the same for every mass. Music for the mass includes the Kyrie, Gloria, Credo, Sanctus, and Agnus Dei as well as other chants, hymns, and psalms. For special mass occasions composers through the centuries have created large musical works for choruses, soloists, instrumentalists, and orchestras.

measure The space from one bar line to the next; also called bars.

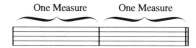

medieval Historical period prior to the Renaissance, c. 500-1450.

medley A group of tunes, linked together and sung consecutively.

melisma (n.) or melismatic (adj.) (muh-LIZ-mah or muh-liz-MAT-ik) [Gk.] A term describing the setting of one syllable of text to several pitches.

melodic interval Intervals that are performed in succession; *see also* harmonic interval.

melody A logical succession of musical tones; also called tune.

meter The pattern into which a steady succession of rhythmic pulses (beats) is organized.

meter signature The divided number at the beginning of a clef; 4/4, 3/4, and so forth; *see also* time signature.

metronome marking A sign that appears over the top line of the treble clef staff at the beginning of a piece indicating the tempo. It shows the kind of note that will get the beat and the numbers of beats per minute as measured by a metronome; for example, ♪ = 100.

mezzo forte (*mf*) (MEHT-soh FOR-teh) [It.] Medium loud.

mezzo piano (*mp*) (MEHT-soh pee-AH-noh) [It.] Medium soft.

middle C   The note that is located nearest the center of the piano keyboard; middle C can be written in either the treble or bass clef.

minor (key, scale)   Scale built on the formula of one whole step, one half step, two whole steps, one half step, two whole steps.

Letter Names:	D	E	F	G	A	Bb	C	D
Movable Do:	la	ti	do	re	mi	fa	so	la
Numbers:	6	7	1	2	3	4	5	6

minor mode   One of two modes upon which the basic scales of Western music are based, the other being major; using W for a whole step and H for a half step, a minor scale has the pattern W H W W H W W.

minor triad   Three tones that form a minor third (bottom) and a major third (top), such as A C E.

minor third   The name for an interval of three half steps. For example, from A to C.

mixed meter   Frequently changing time signatures or meters.

moderato   Moderate.

modulation   Adjusting to a change of keys within a song.

molto   Very or much; for example, *molto rit.* means "much slower."

monophonic   (mah-nuh-FAH-nik) [Gk.] A musical texture having a single melodic line with no accompaniment; monophony.

monophony   (muh-NAH-fuh-nee) [Gk.] One sound; music that has a single melody. Gregorian chants or plainsongs exhibit monophony.

motive   A shortened expression, sometimes contained within a phrase.

musical variations   Changes in rhythm, pitch, dynamics, style, and tempo to create new statements of the established theme.

mysterioso   Perform in a mysterious or haunting way; to create a haunting mood.

N

nationalism   Patriotism; pride of country. This feeling influenced many Romantic composers such as Wagner, Tchaikovsky, Dvořák, Chopin, and Brahms.

natural   (♮) Cancels a previous sharp (♯) lowering the pitch a half step, or a previous flat (♭), raising the pitch a half step.

no breath mark   A direction not to take a breath at a specific place in the composition. (or N.B.)

notation   Written notes, symbols, and directions used to represent music within a composition.

O

octave   An interval of twelve half steps; 8 or 8va = an octave above; 8vb = an octave below.

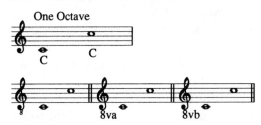

opera   A combination of singing, instrumental music, dancing, and drama that tells a story.

optional divisi   (*opt. div.*) Indicating a split in the music into optional harmony, shown by the smaller cued note.

oratorio   A piece for solo voices, chorus, and orchestra, that is an expanded dramatic work on a literary or religious theme presented without theatrical action.

ostinato   (ahs-tuh-NAH-toh) [It.] A rhythmic or melodic passage that is repeated continuously.

P

palate   The roof of the mouth; the hard palate is forward, the soft palate (velum) is at the back.

parallel major and minor keys   Major and minor keys having the same tonic, such as A major and A minor (A major being the parallel major of A minor and A minor the parallel minor of A major).

peak   The high point in the course of a development; for example, the high point of a musical phrase or the high point in a movement of instrumental music.

pentatonic scale   A five-tone scale constructed of *do, re, mi, so, la* (degrees 1, 2, 3, 5, 6) of a corresponding major scale.

Perfect 5th   The name for an interval of three whole steps and one half step. For example, C to G.

Perfect 4th   The name for an interval of two whole steps and one half step. For example, C to F.

phrase   A musical sentence containing a beginning, middle, and end.

phrase mark   In music, an indicator of the length of a phrase in a melody; this mark may also mean that the singer or musician should not take a breath for the duration of the phrase. (   )

phrasing The realization of the phrase structure of a work; largely a function of a performer's articulation and breathing.

pianissimo (*pp*) (pee-uh-NEE-suh-moh) [It.] Very soft.

piano (*p*) (pee-ANN-noh) [It.] Soft.

Picardy third An interval of a major third used in the final, tonic chord of a piece written in a minor key.

pick-up *See* upbeat.

pitch Sound, the result of vibration; the highness or lowness of a tone, determined by the number of vibrations per second.

piu (pew) [It.] More; for example, *piu forte* means "more loudly."

poco (POH-koh) [It.] Little; for example, *poco dim.* means "a little softer."

poco a poco (POH-koh ah POH-koh) [It.] Little by little; for example, *poco a poco cresc.* means "little by little increase in volume."

polyphony (n.) or polyphonic (adj.) (pah-LIH-fuh-nee or pah-lee-FAH-nik) [Gk.] The term that means that each voice part begins at a different place, is independent and important, and that sections often repeat in contrasting dynamic levels. Poly = many, phony = sounds.

polyrhythmic The simultaneous use of contrasting rhythmic figures.

presto (PREH-stoh) [It.] Very fast.

program music A descriptive style of music composed to relate or illustrate a specific incident, situation, or drama; the form of the piece is often dictated or influenced by the nonmusical program. This style commonly occurs in music composed during the Romantic period. For example, "The Moldau" from *Má Vlast*, by Bedřich Smetana.

progression A succession of two or more pitches or chords; also melodic or harmonic progression.

R

rallentando (*rall.*) (rahl-en-TAHN-doh) [It.] Meaning to "perform more and more slowly." *See also* ritardando.

recitative (res-uh-TAY-teev) [It.] A speechlike style of singing used in opera, oratorio, and cantata.

register, vocal A term used for different parts of a singer's range, such as head register (high notes) and chest register (low notes).

relative major and minor keys The relative minor of any major key or scale, while sharing its key signature and pitches, takes for its tonic the sixth scale degree of that major key or scale. For example, in D major the sixth scale degree is B (or *la* in solfège), *la* then becomes the tonic for B minor.

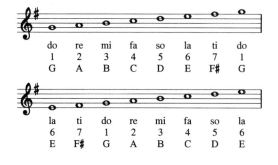

D major   B minor

Renaissance period The historic period in Western Europe from c. 1430 to 1600; the term means "rebirth" or "renewal"; it indicates a period of rapid development in exploration, science, art, and music.

repeat sign A direction to repeat the section of music (‖:‖); if the first half of this sign is omitted, it means to "go back to the beginning" (:‖).

repetition The restatement of a musical idea; repeated pitches; repeated "A" section in ABA form.

resolution (*res.*) A progression from a dissonant tone or harmony to a consonant harmony; a sense of completion.

resonance Reinforcement and intensification of sound by vibrations.

rest Symbols used to indicated silence.

rhythm The pattern of sounds and silences.

rhythmic motif A rhythmic pattern that is repeated throughout a movement or composition.

ritardando (*rit.*) The gradual slowing of tempo; also called "ritard."

Rococo Music of the Baroque period so elaborate it was named after a certain type of fancy rock work.

Romantic period A historic period starting c. 1820 and ending c. 1900 in which artists and composers attempted to break with classical music ideas.

rondo form An instrumental form based on an alternation between a repeated (or recurring) section and contrasting episodes (ABACADA).

root The bottom note of a triad in its original position; the note on which the chord is built.

round A composition in which the perpetual theme (sometimes with harmonic parts) begins in one group and is strictly imitated in other groups in an overlapping fashion. Usually the last voice to enter becomes the final voice to complete the song.

rubato (roo-BAH-toh) [It.] Freely; allows the conductor or the performer to vary the tempo.

S

sacred music Of or dealing with religious music; hymns, chorales, early masses; *see* secular music.

scale A pattern of pitches arranged by whole steps and half steps.

	do	re	mi	fa	so	la	ti	do
	1	2	3	4	5	6	7	1
	G	A	B	C	D	E	F♯	G

	la	ti	do	re	mi	fa	so	la
	6	7	1	2	3	4	5	6
	E	F♯	G	A	B	C	D	E

score The arrangement of instrumental and vocal staffs that all sound at the same time.

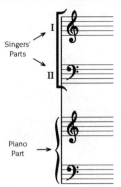

secular music Music without religious content; *see* sacred music.

sempre (SEHM-preh) [It.] Always, continually.

sequence Repetition of a pattern of notes on a higher or lower pitch level.

sharp A symbol (accidental) that raises a pitch by one half step. (♯)

sight-sing Reading and singing of music at first sight.

simile (*sim.*) (SIM-ee-leh) [It.] To continue in the same way.

simple meter Meter in which each beat is divisible by 2.

skip Melodic movement in intervals larger than a whole step.

slur Curved line placed over or under a group of notes to indicate that they are to be performed without a break. (⌒)

solfège (SOHL-fehj) [Fr.] A method of sight-singing, using the syllables *do, re, mi, fa, so, la, ti*, etc. for pitches of the scale.

solo Composition for one featured performer.

sonata-allegro form (suh-NAH-tuh ah-LEH-groh) [It.] Large A B A form consisting of three sections: exposition, development, and recapitulation.

soprano The higher female voice.

sotto voce In a quiet, subdued manner; "under" the voice.

spirito (SPEE-ree-toh) [It.] Spirited; for example, *con spirito*, with spirit.

spiritual A type of song created by African Americans who combined African rhythms with melodies they created and heard in America.

staccato (stah-KAH-toh) [It.] Performed in a short, detached manner, as opposed to legato.

staff Series of five horizontal lines and four spaces on which music is written to show pitch.

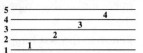

staggered entrances Voice parts or instruments begin singing or playing at different points within the composition.

steady beat A metrical pulse; *see also* beat, meter, rhythm.

step Melodic movement from one note to the next adjacent note, either higher or lower.

stepwise melodic movement Motion from one note to an adjacent one.

stress Emphasis on certain notes or rhythmic elements.

strong beat Naturally accented beats; beats 1 and 3 in 4/4 meter, beat 1 in 3/4 meter.

strophic Description of a song in which all the stanzas of the text are sung to the same music; opposite of *through-composed*.

style The particular character of a musical work; often indicated by words at the beginning of a composition, telling the performer the general manner in which the piece is to be performed.

subito (sub.) (SOO-bee-toh) [It.] Suddenly; for example, *sub. piano* means "suddenly soft."

suspension or suspended tone The tone or tones in a chord that are held as the remainder of the notes change to a new chord. The sustained tones often form a *dissonance* with the new chord, into which they then resolve.

sustained tone A tone sustained in duration; sometimes implying a slowing of tempo; *sostenuto* or *sostenendo*, abbreviated *sost*.

swing This is a performance style in which a pair of eighth notes (♫) are no longer performed evenly, but instead like a triplet (♩♪), yet they are still written (♫); usually indicated at the beginning of a song or a section.

symphony An extended work in several movements, for orchestra; also an orchestra configured to perform symphonic music.

syncopation Deliberate shifts of accent so that a rhythm goes against the steady beat; sometimes referred to as the "offbeat."

T

tempo   A pace with which music moves, based on the speed of the underlying beat.

tempo I or tempo primo   Return to the first tempo.

tenor   A high male voice, lower than the alto, but higher than bass.

tenuto   (teh-NOO-toh) [It.] Stress and extend the marked note. ($\bar{\rho}$)

text   Words, usually set in a poetic style, that express a central thought, idea, moral, or narrative.

texture   The thickness of the different layers of horizontal and vertical sounds.

theme and variation form   A musical form in which variations of the basic theme comprise the composition.

tie   A curved line connecting two successive notes of the same pitch, indicating that the second note is not to be articulated. (ρ⌒ρ)

timbre   Tone color; the unique quality produced by a voice or instrument.

time signature   The sign placed at the beginning and within a composition to indicate the meter; for example, 4/4, 3/4; *see also* cut time, meter signature.

to coda   Skip to the ⊕ or CODA.

tonality   The organized relationships of pitches with reference to a definite key center. In Western music, most tonalities are organized by the major and minor scales.

tone   A sound quality of a definite pitch.

tone color, quality, or timbre   That which distinguishes the voice or tone of one singer or instrument from another; for example, a soprano from an alto or a flute from a clarinet.

tonic chord   (TAH-nik kord) [Gk.] The name of a chord built on the tonal center of a scale; for example, C E G or *do, mi, so* for C major.

tonic or tonal center   The most important pitch in a scale; *do*; the home tone; the tonal center or root of a key or scale.

tonic triad   A three-note chord comprising root, third, and fifth; for example, C E G.

treble clef   The symbol that appears at the beginning of the staff used for higher voices, instruments, or the piano right hand; generally referring to pitches above middle C, it wraps around the line for G, therefore it is also called the G-clef.

triad   A three-note chord built in thirds above a root tone.

trill   A rapid change between the marked note and the one above it within the same key. (*tr*⌇)

triplet   A group of notes in which three notes of equal duration are sung in the time normally given to two notes of equal duration.

troubadour   A wandering minstrel of noble birth in southern France, Spain, and Italy during the eleventh to thirteenth centuries.

tuning   The process of adjusting the tones of voices or instruments so they will sound the proper pitches.

tutti   (TOO-tee) [It.] Meaning "all" or "together."

twelve-tone music   Twentieth-century system of writing music in which the twelve tones of the chromatic scale are arranged into a tone row (numbered 1 to 12), and then the piece is composed by arranging and rearranging the "row" in different ways; for example, backward, forward, or in clusters of three or four pitches.

U

unison   Voice parts or instruments sounding the same pitches in the same rhythm simultaneously.

upbeat   A weak beat preceding the downbeat.

V

variation   *See* theme and variation form, musical variations.

vivace   (vee-VAH-chay) [It.] Very fast; lively.

voice crossing (or voice exchange)   When one voice "crosses" above or below another voice part.

W

whole step   The combination of two successive half steps. (⌊_⌋)

whole tone scale   A scale consisting only of whole steps.

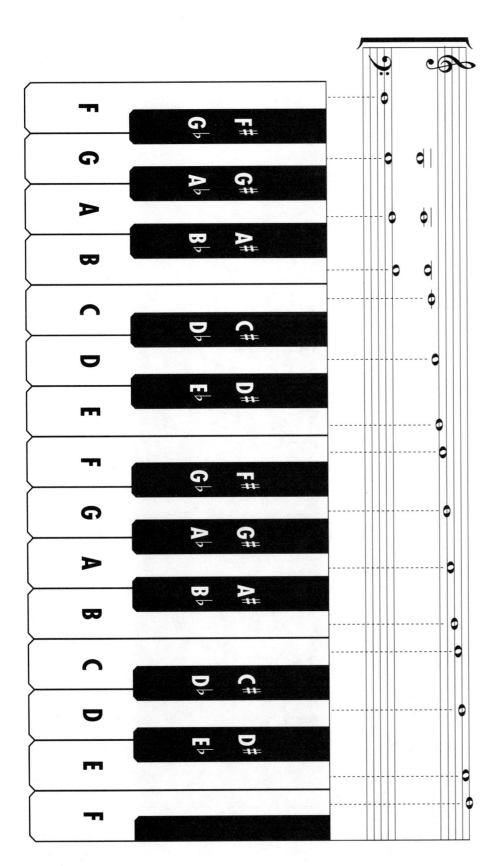

For use with Sight-Singing exercises. Use the keyboard and notation on this page to identify and perform the notes in your voice part.